NAṢĪR AL-DĪN ṬŪSĪ

A PHILOSOPHER FOR ALL SEASONS

Similar Titles Available
From The Islamic Texts Society

Ibn ʿArabī: The Voyage Of No Return

NAṢĪR AL-DĪN ṬŪSĪ

A PHILOSOPHER FOR ALL SEASONS

SAYEH MEISAMI

THE ISLAMIC TEXTS SOCIETY

This edition published in 2019 by
The Islamic Texts Society
Miller's House
Kings Mill Lane
Great Shelford
Cambridge CB22 5EN, U.K.

British Library Cataloguing-in-Publication Data.
A catalogue record for this book is
available from the British Library.

ISBN: 978 1911141 235 paper

Contents

Introduction

Late medieval and early modern portraits of Khwāja Naṣīr al-Dīn Ṭūsī (d. 672/1274) picture him in a position of grandeur either in the company of the Mongol warlord Hulagu Khan (d. 663/1265) or in a circle of other scientists who seem humbled by his presence. Ṭūsī was of the generations of philosopher-scientists who were sought after and supported by the powerful because of their talent and perseverance in generating both theoretical and practical knowledge. Knowledge produced and systematically recorded by a dedicated and professional polymath such as Ṭūsī was an invaluable asset to any institution that was growing in power. In this respect, one can hardly make a distinction between exact sciences and speculative ones. Ṭūsī the philosopher and religious scholar was as valuable to his patrons as Ṭūsī the mathematician and astronomer. Throughout his prolific career, Ṭūsī enjoyed a significant amount of institutional support to carry out his diverse projects and was patronized by both the Ismaʿilis in Persia and the Mongol conquerors. In this light, the moniker 'a philosopher for all seasons' is not only intended as a laudatory epithet but as a reminder of the pragmatic flexibility of Ṭūsī and his ability to mould circumstances in ways that would benefit his perpetual search after knowledge and his numerous ventures.

One could also read the above epithet in the sense of a *philosopher* for all seasons. While delving into almost all the intellectual disciplines of his day, Ṭūsī always remains a philosopher arguing within Peripatetic (*mashshā'ī*) conceptual frameworks; and this, despite his various writings being also informed by Ismaʿili, Illuminationist (*ishrāqī*), Qur'anic and Sufi themes. The force of his philosophical pen, however, is to be felt more in his synthetic interpretations and critical perspectives rather than in his original philosophical ideas. Compared to Ibn Sīnā and Suhrawardī—who were his major inspirations—he did not establish ground-breaking philosophical narratives. For example, Ṭūsī's famous treatise on Twelver theology, *Tajrīd al-iʿtiqād* (The Summa of the Dogma), is written within the philosophical framework of Ibn Sīnā, using technical philosophical language and specialized axioms. In the same vein, his works on ethics, politics and even Sufism are strongly coloured by concepts and themes from Peripatetic and Illuminationist philosophies that are, in turn, rooted in the philosophies of Plato and Aristotle. Nonetheless, in his commentaries on Ibn Sīnā and Suhrawardī's ideas and in his borrowings from them, Ṭūsī has his own voice and offers new perspectives on old positions. This extends, as will be explained later in this book, to Ṭūsī's Ismaʿili treatises, in which one can find an interesting array of philosophical ideas that he uses to rationalize Ismaʿili doctrines.

Ṭūsī's life was an eventful one due to the historical and social conditions of his time, as well as his wholehearted will to live a full, ambitious life. While his first major migration found him seeking refuge with the Ismaʿilis from the Mongol invasions, three decades later, his second important journey was in the company of the Mongol warlord Hulagu towards the Abbasid Baghdad, which was about to fall to the invaders. Regardless of Ṭūsī's contribution to the outcome of major events in his time, the fact that he was witness to them crucially demonstrates how one of the most tumultuous periods in medieval Muslim history affected the intellectual productions of an influential figure who was both impacted by the events and contributed to them. In fact, some of Ṭūsī's writings exemplify conversations between philosophy and history, which then highlight the intricate relationship between the life of the mind and socio-political realities.

A Rising Star in Khurāsān

Muḥammad b. Muḥammad b. al-Ḥasan al-Ṭūsī was born into a Twelver Shiʿa (*ithnā ʿasharī*) family on a Saturday in 597/1201, in the small city of Ṭūs in the province of Khurāsān in the north-east of Iran. Along with the celebrated Persian poet of the fourth/tenth century Abu'l-Qāsim Firdawsī (d. 411/1020 or 416/1025), Abū Ḥāmid Muḥammad Ghazālī (d. 505/1111), and several other men of letters, Ṭūsī guaranteed that the name of this city remain noted in intellectual history. All we know about Ṭūsī's childhood is that his father, who was an established Twelver religious scholar, exposed him to the sciences of the time especially religious sciences from an early age. This shows that Ṭūsī's childhood must have been a quiet one and that he was both very talented and eager to learn. Like his past master Ibn Sīnā, Ṭūsī was privileged in having a supportive family, which helped him take his first steps smoothly towards a prolific academic career.[1]

As a young scholar, Ṭūsī moved to Nishāpūr, the clos-

1 For Ṭūsī's life, see Muḥammad Taqī Mudarris Raḍawī, *Aḥwāl wa-āthār-i qudwa-yi muḥaqqiqīn wa-ṣulṭān-i ḥukamā wa-mutakallimīn ustād-i bashar wa-ʿaql-i ḥādī al-ʿashar Abū Jaʿfar Muḥammad b. Muḥammad b. al-Ḥasan al-Ṭūsī mulaqqab bih Naṣīr al-Dīn*, Tehran: Chāpkhāna-yi dāwarpanāh wa khwājah, 1354/1976, pp. 3–64.

est centre of learning to his hometown Ṭūs, which could no longer meet his demands for more advanced studies. In his spiritual autobiography, *Sayr wa-sulūk* (Contemplation and Action), Ṭūsī mentions that he moved from his hometown after the death of his father 'in search of the truth, intending to acquire the knowledge that guides people to the happiness of the next world.'[1] Nishāpūr has a special place in Persian collective memory due to its raising and hosting of great scholars and the earliest institutions of learning since the Sassanid era, as well as the tragedies that befell the city during the Mongol invasion. When Ṭūsī arrived in Nishāpūr, the city was still an active academic centre with scholars from numerous fields. Ṭūsī managed to study with many of the well-known scholars of the city. For example, he learned philosophy from Farīd al-Dīn Dāmād Nishāpūrī, whose philosophical knowledge is believed to have come from Ibn Sīnā through the chain of four other identified philosophers. This early philosophical education in the school of Ibn Sīnā explains Ṭūsī's lifelong dedication to Avicennan philosophy, which is illustrated not only by his long commentary on Ibn Sīnā's *al-Ishārāt wa'l-tanbīhāt* (The Pointers and Reminders) but also by most of his other works including his metaphysical, theological, ethical, political and spiritual treatises. In Nishāpūr, Ṭūsī also immersed himself in the study of Islamic Twelver jurisprudence (*fiqh*), mathematics and medicine.[2]

Life and Work in Isma^cili Fortresses

Ṭūsī's life as a carefree youth committed only to studying was interrupted around 624/1226 by the fear of the imminent attack of the Mongols on north-east Persia. His

1 Naṣīr al-Dīn Ṭūsī, *Sayr wa-sulūk*, trans. S. J. Badakhchani as *Contemplation and Action*, London & New York: I. B. Tauris, 1998, p. 27.
2 Raḍawī, *Aḥwāl wa-āthār*, p. 6.

choice to move away from Nishāpūr was wise as, when they took the city, the Mongol swords made no distinction between scholars and peasants. Moreover, at that time he had already received an offer from the Isma῾ili chief Nāṣir al-Dīn ῾Abd al-Raḥīm b. Abī Manṣūr (d. 655/1257)—who held the honorific title of Muḥtasham (Chief)—to move to the Isma῾ili fortress in Quhistān, south of Khurāsān, which was not only safe but could provide Ṭūsī with the means to further his studies. Ṭūsī's migration to Quhistān was the beginning of a very prolific period of his intellectual life, but a period that also gave rise to many controversies about his religious and political affiliations. Nāṣir al-Dīn Muḥtasham was himself a learned person and a patron of the sciences. He encouraged Ṭūsī to write two major books on ethics, one of which was originally outlined by the Muḥtasham himself, who also contributed to it during Ṭūsī's completion of the manuscript. Both books were dedicated to Nāṣir al-Dīn ῾Abd al-Raḥīm b. Abī Manṣūr and carry his name in their titles. The larger, and more popular of the two books, is *Akhlāq-i Nāṣirī* (The Nasirean Ethics).[1] It is a translation into Persian and summary with additional comments of an earlier Arabic book on ethics by the Persian philosopher Ibn Miskawayh (d. 421/1030). Apart from its profound content and innovative approach to ethics, the book is also important because it was written in Persian. Writing in Persian, Ṭūsī became one of the forerunners of those producing Islamic intellectual texts in a language other than Arabic. The content of the book will be discussed later under the section on ethics. The earlier version of the preamble (*dībācha*) of the book contains many compliments to Nāṣir al-Dīn Muḥtasham

1 Naṣīr al-Dīn Ṭūsī, *Akhlāq-i Nāṣirī*, trans. G. M. Wickens as *The Nasirean Ethics*, London & New York: Routledge, 1964.

and includes ideas taken from Isma'ili ideology; however, years later after leaving the Isma'ili fortress, Ṭūsī changed the preamble by omitting the compliments.[1]

The other book that Ṭūsī wrote for the Muḥtasham is titled *Akhlāq-i Muḥtashamī* (The Ethics of the Muḥtasham). In the preamble of the book, Ṭūsī explains that Nāṣir al-Dīn Muḥtasham had previously gathered thoughts on virtuous conduct from the Qur'an, Traditions (*ḥadīth*) and the words of Isma'ili summoners (*du'āt*)[2] but had never managed to complete the task of writing the book due to the demands of his office as a governor. In this work, Ṭūsī calls the Muḥtasham 'the reservoir of wisdom and source of mercy' and says that while writing the book he incorporated the Muḥtasham's own words and comments.[3] In comparison with *Akhlāq-i Nāṣirī*, *Akhlāq-i Muḥtashamī* has a stronger religious and spiritual tone, and its forty chapters are intended to guide the seeker after happiness through forty days of spiritual striving. Among the sources used in writing this book, the *Nahj al-balāgha* of 'Alī b. Abī Ṭālib and *al-Ṣaḥīfa al-sajjādiyya* by 'Alī b. al-Ḥusayn Zayn al-'Ābidīn have been identified by the contemporary editor of the text, Muḥammad Ṭaqī Dānishpazhūh.[4]

During his stay in Quhistān between 624/1226-632/1234, Ṭūsī wrote several other works including a treatise on astronomy that he dedicated to the Muḥtasham's son Mu'īn al-Dīn. Among his other treatises believed to have been

1 Raḍawī, *Aḥwāl wa-āthār*, p. 452.

2 A summoner (*dā'ī*) was an Isma'ili missionary.

3 Ibid., p. 559.

4 Hamid Dabashi, 'Khwājah Naṣīr al-Dīn Ṭūsī: the Philosopher/Vizier and the Intellectual Climate of his Times', in Seyyed Hossein Nasr and Oliver Leaman, eds., *History of Islamic Philosophy*, London & New York: Routledge, 1996, vol. II, p. 559.

written during this time too is *Tawallā wa-tabarrā* (Solidarity and Dissociation), which is based on Isma^cili themes. It is thought he started his autobiography, *Sayr wa-sulūk*, about the same time, as well as his famous commentary on Ibn Sīnā's *al-Ishārāt wa'l-tanbīhāt*.[1]

Around 632/1234, Ṭūsī was invited to the fortress of Alamūt in Rūdbār and he stayed there until the Mongol invasion of 1256; it was one of the most prolific periods of his life. Alamūt was the heartland of the Ismaʿili territories in Persia and at the time was under the imamate of ʿAlā' al-Dīn Muḥammad (d. 653/1255) and then of Rukn al-Dīn Khurshāh (d. 654/1256), whose rule was cut short by the Mongols. Ṭūsī served both Ismaʿili imams in Alamūt. There he completed his commentary on *al-Ishārāt wa'l-tanbīhāt*, and several Ismaʿili treatises, including *Rawḍa-yi taslīm* (The Paradise of Submission), which is attributed to Ṭūsī in co-authorship with the Ismaʿili summoner and poet Ḥasan-i Maḥmūd, Ṭūsī's advisor on Ismaʿili thought in Alamūt.[2] This treatise is a philosophical presentation of Ismaʿili doctrines that will be discussed later in this book.

There are different views on Ṭūsī's life among the Ismaʿilis and whether he stayed in their fortresses for three decades voluntarily or against his will. There is really no way of knowing how he actually felt about his life there or whether he really converted to the Ismaʿili faith as he alludes to in his autobiography. But we know that his intellectual life flourished during his stay with the Ismaʿilis

1 S. J. Badakhchani, *Shiʿī Interpretations of Islam*, London & New York: I. B. Tauris, 2010, pp. 4–5.

2 S. J. Badakhchani, Preface to Naṣīr al-Dīn Ṭūsī, *Paradise of Submission: A Medieval Treatise on Ismaili Thought*, ed. and trans. S. J. Badakhchani, London: I. B. Tauris in association with the Institute of Ismaili Studies, 2005, p. xvi.

and due to their patronage. He had a relatively quiet life for over three decades until the arrival of Hulagu and the Mongols in Rūdbār in early 654/1256.

The previous year, Nāṣir al-Dīn Muḥtasham, who was Ṭūsī's first Ismaᶜili patron, surrendered to Hulagu and advised him that his complete victory over the Ismaᶜili territories would depend on Rukn al-Dīn Khurshāh. He was awarded for his surrender with the governance of Ṭūn, which had been destroyed by the Mongols. He died shortly thereafter. The Mongols advanced on the Ismaᶜili fortresses of Rūdbār and Daylamān with an entourage of both military and Persian scholarly figures whom they had recruited during their earlier conquests. Among these figures was the celebrated historian ᶜAṭā Malik Juwaynī, who wrote a chronicle of the Mongol conquests in Persian known as *Tārīkh-i jahāngushāy* (A History of a World Conqueror) based on his own eyewitness account. Hulagu started negotiations with Rukn al-Dīn Khurshāh. After several complications in the negotiations due to Khurshāh's postponement in surrendering, Hulagu launched an attack on Rūdbār in mid-654/1256. Finally, in 29 Shawwāl 654/19 November 1256 Khurshāh appeared outside the fortress to declare his surrender; with him was a large group of his family and companions including Ṭūsī. This marked the end of 166 years of Ismaᶜili rule in that region.[1] According to the testimony of Juwaynī himself, he pleaded with Hulagu to salvage some of the valuable books and astronomical devices from the Alamūt library before it was set on fire.[2] This was the library that provided Ṭūsī with his resources,

1 Farhad Daftary, *The Ismāᶜīlīs: Their History and Doctrines*, Cambridge: Cambridge University Press, 1990, p. 395.

2 ᶜAṭā Malik Juwaynī, *Tārīkh-i jahāngushāy*, ed. Muḥammad b. ᶜAbd al-Wahhāb Qazwīnī, Leiden: Brill, 1911, vol. III, p. 270.

especially the intellectual works by Fatimid thinkers such as Ḥamīd al-Dīn Kirmānī (d. 412/1021) and Nāṣir-i Khusraw (d. after 469/1077). One cannot say with certainty if it was Ṭūsī who persuaded Juwaynī to save the books, but the possibility is not far-fetched. Also, it is not clear if Ṭūsī had an effective role in encouraging Khurshāh to surrender but based on his later closeness to Hulagu and his keen survival instinct, it is a reasonable conclusion. Moreover, the fact that Hulagu trusted Ṭūsī from the very beginning suggests that he must have believed Ṭūsī had had a role in the surrender of the fortress.

A Warlord's Confidant and Astronomer

After the fall of the Ismaᶜili fortresses, Ṭūsī's life enters a different phase. From the quiet life of a scholar-in-residence among the Ismaᶜilis, Ṭūsī's role shifted to that of advisor to a warlord whose dream was to conquer the capital of the Abbasid caliphate. Within two years of joining the circle of Hulagu's confidants, Ṭūsī witnessed the fall of Baghdad, and there are different narratives about his role in the event. The details of the siege of Baghdad are recorded in an appendix to Juwaynī's *Tārīkh-i jahāngushāy*; this appendix is attributed to Ṭūsī. The tone of the appendix is of total approval of the siege and sack of Baghdad and refers to the Abbasids as the enemy. But there is no direct mention of Ṭūsī's role in the event. Most historians believe that Hulagu took Ṭūsī's advice during the siege and that he was one of Hulagu's main envoys in his negotiations with the Caliph. After the fall of the city, which was soon followed by the execution of the Caliph, Ṭūsī was commanded by Hulagu to write a letter of victory (*fatḥ-nāma*) that was sent to the governors of Syria.[1] Although the attack on Baghdad caused considerable destruction, some of the institutions of learning, most prominently the Niẓāmiyya, were to be renovated by Juwaynī, who was supported in this by Hulagu.[2] Whatever the extent of his contribution to the Abbasids' demise, Ṭūsī must have gained the trust of his Mongol patron during the siege since Hulagu accepted his pleading for the lives of some of the intellectual elite of Baghdad. It is also reported that around this time Ṭūsī converted Hulagu and his family to Islam.

Once in Baghdad, Ṭūsī returns to the faith of his ancestors, Twelver Shiʿism, and spends the rest of his life serving its cause.[3] His first step was to visit Ḥilla, which was the centre of learning for Twelver Shiʿa scholars in Iraq. In Ḥilla, Ṭūsī was regarded with respect by its scholars; especially so by the famous Twelver theologian ʿAllāma Ibn Muṭahhar al-Ḥillī (d. 726/1325). This demonstrates that Twelver authorities did not doubt that, as Ṭūsī had claimed at the time of his surrender to Hulagu, he had been forced to serve the Ismaʿilis; or they simply chose to believe this given Ṭūsī's high intellectual and political status. Ḥillī's commentary on Ṭūsī's major theological treatise *Tajrīd al-iʿtiqād*—which Ṭūsī completed under the patronage of the Mongols—was to become essential to understanding Ṭūsī's theological positions.

As for Hulagu, what interested him most in Ṭūsī's intel-

1 The victory letter is fully quoted by Mudarris Raḍawī, *Aḥwāl wa-āthār*, pp. 28–31.

2 Dabashi, 'Khwājah Naṣīr al-Dīn Ṭūsī', p. 540.

3 The first point of divergence between Twelvers and Ismaʿilis is that the former acknowledged the imamate of Mūsā al-Kāẓim as the successor of Jaʿfar al-Ṣādiq, while the latter chose his brother Ismāʿīl, hence the title 'Ismaʿilis'.

lectual output was the latter's astronomical projects. The establishment of the Marāgha Observatory in north-west Iran is often mentioned as one of the highlights of Ṭūsī's career. There are different stories about the origin of the idea behind building the observatory. But there is a strong possibility that Hulagu had considered Ṭūsī's potential for achieving this goal before he decided to keep him in his company after the conquest of the Ismaʿili fortresses. Some narratives depict Ṭūsī as trying hard to convince Hulagu to fund his costly project. Considering the time and expense that were required for completing the project, Hulagu's original reluctance cannot be easily dismissed, but it is less likely than his enthusiasm for supporting it. Moreover, Hulagu had great trust in Ṭūsī's decisions and the observatory would be home to a circle of great minds of the age. Having such a scientific institution to his credit would be a great achievement for a commander and Hulagu must have been pleased to receive Ṭūsī's proposal.

The construction of the Marāgha Observatory began in 657/1259. Ṭūsī's scientific authority attracted established scientists and mathematicians to Marāgha and they remained to work together in Ṭūsī's circle for many years. These scholars included Quṭb al-Dīn Shīrāzī, Shams al-Dīn Shirwānī, Muḥyī al-Dīn al-Maghribī, Farīd al-Dīn b. Fawṭī, Kamāl al-Dīn 'Ījī, Mu'ayyid al-Dīn al-ʿUrḍī, Fakhr al-Dīn Marāghī, Fakhr al-Dīn Akhlāṭī, and Najm al-Dīn Dabīrān Kātibī. In his preface to the *Ilkhānī zīj*, which is an incomplete table of astronomical observations and predications (*zīj*) dedicated to their Mongol patron (*Ilkhān*), Ṭūsī only mentions the last four scholars by name, which later caused resentment among those whom he had not mentioned. Among the people who worked with Ṭūsī, there were also a number of Chinese astronomers. It is believed that these Chinese astronomers came west with Hulagu. If this is the case, then Hulagu may already have had a plan for funding scientific projects before he even met Ṭūsī. The scientists mentioned above were hired to both construct the observatory and its astronomical tools, as well as to perform and record astronomical observations. Most importantly, their collaboration was the foundation of an influential academic circle in Marāgha, which also resulted in the establishment of a resource library. In addition to state funding, the observatory also relied on widespread fundraising and donations, including religious endowments collected by Hulagu's agents from different cities. Ṭūsī's last writings, most prominently his *Tadhkira fī ʿilm al-hay'a* (Memoir on the Science of Astronomy), all address the scientific achievements of Marāgha.[1]

Ṭūsī lived longer than Hulagu and witnessed the era of Hulagu's successor, Abqā' Khan (ruled 663/1265-680/1282), for whom he worked as court physician. Like Hulagu, Abqā' respected and supported Ṭūsī, and the observatory was still active under his rule. Ṭūsī even wrote a medical book about facts and manners of sexual intimacy at the request of Abqā' Khan and dedicated the book to him.[2] There are a number of accounts of Ṭūsī's medical practice at Abqā''s court especially his treatment of the Khan himself. But during this time, Ṭūsī himself was in his old age and suffering from an illness. Despite this, in the years prior to his death, Ṭūsī was still active and travelled to several cities, including Quhistān and Baghdad, on both academic and administrative missions. In the year 672/1274, in Baghdad,

1 See Ṭūsī, *Tadhkira fī ʿilm al-hay'a*, trans. F. J. Ragep as *Naṣīr al-Dīn Ṭūsī's Memoir on Astronomy*, Norman, Oklahoma: University of Oklahoma, 1993.
2 Ṭūsī, *al-Bāb al-bāhiya fī'l-tarākib al-sulṭāniyya*, ed. and trans. Daniel L. Newman as *The Sultan's Sex Potion,* London: Saqi Books, 2014.

he finally succumbed to his illness. During his last days, he wrote his last will and testament and asked to be buried at the site of the mausoleum of the seventh Shiʿa imam, Mūsā al-Kāẓim (d. 183/799) in Kāẓimiyya, Iraq. His insistence on being buried there can be interpreted as a final attempt to prove to his peers his allegiance to the Twelver faith. Ṭūsī had several children but, as in the case of most medieval histories and biographies, only the lives of his male descendants were recorded. His three sons, Ṣadr al-Dīn ʿAlī, Aṣīl al-Dīn Ḥasan and Fakhr al-Dīn Aḥmad, led eventful lives of their own as they were engaged in both the politics and the academic affairs of the day. Their descendants are also reported to have held high offices in the court of the Safavids.[1] Ṭūsī remained popular under the Safavids and was praised by famous Safavid figures such as Bahā' al-Dīn al-ʿĀmilī (d. 984/1576) and Muḥammad Bāqir Majlisī (d. 1110/1698);[2] he continues to be popular in contemporary Iran.

To sum up, Ṭūsī lived a very productive life as a philosopher and scientist. He was fortunate in that the social and political crises of his time did not interrupt his intellectual activities. In the many fields that he contributed to, Ṭūsī was a link between what went before him and an influence on what came after him. In philosophy, he was the continuation of the two most significant philosophical traditions in the Muslim world, the Peripatetics and the Illuminationists. In the sciences, he was the link between the Hellenic world, including the astronomy of Ptolemy and the mathematics of Euclid, and Renaissance-era mathematicians and astronomers such as Copernicus.

Ṭūsī's intellectual production will be discussed under two major categories of theoretical and practical wisdom.

1 Raḍawī, *Aḥwāl wa-āthār*, pp. 68–77.

2 Ibid., pp. 89–90.

This is only a pedagogical division, for the character of Ṭūsī's thought is much more holistic. The chapter on theoretical wisdom includes Ṭūsī's metaphysics, theory of knowledge, theology, logic, and exact sciences. The chapter on practical wisdom includes ethics, economics, aesthetics and politics with the latter including his theory of the Shiʿa imamate. Finally, I shall also discuss Ṭūsī's contribution to Sufism, poetry and music.

CHAPTER ONE

Theoretical Wisdom

While Ṭūsī produced his philosophical texts within Ibn Sīnā's conceptual framework, he also relied on two other speculative traditions—the Illuminationist philosophy of Shihāb al-Dīn Suhrawardī (d. 587/1191) and Ismaʿilism. As much of the discussion below will focus on Ṭūsī's reliance on Ibn Sīnā, it is important to alert the reader from the start to the influences also of Suhrawardī and Ismaʿilism on his thought and output. There are several places in Ṭūsī's works where the influence of Suhrawardī is obvious, most prominently in his theory of divine knowledge, which will be discussed later in the book. Suhrawardī must have appealed to Ṭūsī on two counts. First, Ṭūsī must have sensed a wind of change in Suhrawardī's daring use of ancient pre-Socratic and Persian narratives, not to mention a restoration of ideas that had been forgotten under the hegemony of the Peripatetic discourse. In this spirit, like Suhrawardī, Ṭūsī contributed to the tradition of producing intellectual texts in Persian and wrote some of his major works in his native language, which set an example for his students and colleagues, including the famous philosopher and scientist Quṭb al-Dīn Shīrāzī (d. 710/1311). The second reason for Ṭūsī's attraction to Suhrawardī must have been the esoteric character of the latter's thought and the possibility of interpreting some aspects of his philosophy, especially his political philosophy, in a Shiʿa light. Although he does not comment on the possibility of reading Suhrawardī from an Ismaʿili perspective, he could not have missed the Shiʿa undertones of Suhrawardī's writings.

Regarding the Ismaʿili influence, apart from Ṭūsī's earlier writings written during his long residence in Ismaʿili fortresses and apart from his focus on Ismaʿili themes, there are also traces of Ismaʿili narratives in his other works. It would be methodologically wrong to ignore or underestimate Ṭūsī's Ismaʿili writings on the pretext of dubious authorship, which has been overemphasized by some Twelver scholars. In addition to his autobiography, which offers strong textual evidence for his attraction to Ismaʿili philosophy, his major work on ethics *Akhlāq-i Nāṣirī* (Nasirean Ethics) also shows the influence of Ismaʿili thought.[1] Herman Landolt adds to this list Ṭūsī's commentary on Ibn Sīnā's *al-Ishārāt wa'l-tanbīhāt*,[2] which will be discussed below. There seems to be no justification for accepting the latter two as free expressions of his own thought while dismissing the autobiography as forced on him by his Ismaʿili patrons. Whether Ṭūsī did or did not genuinely convert to Ismaʿilism does not alter the presence of Ismaʿili concepts and narratives in his writings. The fact that Ṭūsī spent three decades of his life among Ismaʿilis, studied their texts and composed some of his major works in conversation with them is a strong

1 On this subject, see Wilferd Madelung, 'Naṣīr al-Dīn Ṭūsī's Ethics between Philosophy, Shiʿism, and Sufism', in Paul Luft and Colin Turner, eds., *Shiʿism*, London & New York: Routledge, 2008, vol. II, pp. 69–85.

2 Herman Landolt, 'Kwājah Naṣīr al-Dīn Ṭūsī, Ismaʿīlism and Ishrāqī Philosophy', in N. Pourjavady and Ž. Vesel, eds., *Naṣīr al-Dīn Ṭūsī Philosophe et Savant du XIIIe Siècle*, Tehran: Institut Français de Recherche en Iran, 2000, pp. 13–30.

motivation to pay attention to Ismaʿili connections at least in those of his works that do not have an outright Twelver theological focus.

It is important to note the centrality of the esoteric perspective for Ṭūsī; it may explain his leanings towards philosophy as opposed to theology *per se* and place his attraction to both the Illuminationist school and Ismaʿilism within his overall conceptual framework.

Exoteric and Esoteric

In his autobiography *Sayr wa-sulūk*, Ṭūsī states that truth is in the possession of esoterists (*ahl al-bāṭin*) rather than exoterists (*ahl al-ẓāhir*).[1] Ṭūsī depicts his own spiritual and intellectual life as a journey from the exoteric (*ẓāhir*) to the esoteric (*bāṭin*). He uses these binary concepts in accordance with their meanings in Ismaʿili discourses. Broadly construed, Ismaʿili thinkers make a distinction between two levels of understanding: the exoteric, which is based on the literal meaning of religious texts as well as the apparent or physical layer of the cosmos, and the esoteric, which discloses the hidden meanings of religious texts and the cosmos through spiritual interpretation (*taʾwīl*). For example, regarding those who possess esoteric knowledge, the Fatimid jurisprudent and judge Qāḍī al-Nuʿmān (d. 363/974) holds the Shiʿa imams to be the most authoritative sources of this knowledge; and this is reinforced by their immunity (*ʿiṣma*) from sin and errors of judgement.[2]

In *Sayr wa-sulūk*, Ṭūsī calls exoterists (*ahl al-ẓāhir*) 'those who blindly follow the rules of the *Sharīʿa* (the religious law).' He also expresses his disappointment with dialecti-

1 Ṭūsī, *Contemplation and Action*, p. 27.

2 Abū Ḥanīfa al-Nuʿmān, *Asās al-taʾwīl*, ed. Aref Tamer, Beirut: Manshūrāt Dār al-Thaqāfa, 1960, p. 66.

cal theology (*kalām*) because 'its practitioners seemed to force the intellect to promote a doctrine in which they blindly imitated their ancestors,' and in contrast he regards philosophy (*ʿilm-i ḥikmat*) as noble (*sharīf*) for the liberty it gives to the intellect and the avoidance of blind imitation (*taqlīd*).[1] Thus, as a philosopher, Ṭūsī locates the activity of the intellect closer to esoterism, though he does not identify philosophy as the ultimate venue of certain knowledge. While appreciating the value of philosophy, he denounces the intellectual hubris of those who consider their human intellect as self-sufficient. Notwithstanding, he admits that he himself has benefited from philosophers and he freely adopts their philosophical tools to develop the main theme of his autobiography, namely the Ismaʿili doctrine of instruction (*taʿlīm*).

Instruction (*taʿlīm*), as systematically formulated by Ḥasan-i Ṣabbāḥ (d. 518/1124), the founder of the Nizārī community in northern Persia, is the central doctrine of Nizārī Ismaʿilism. Due to the significance of this doctrine for them, the Nizārīs are also referred to as the 'people of instruction' (*Taʿlīmiyya*). According to this doctrine, the attainment of true knowledge is only possible through the instruction of the imam or, in the imam's absence, his representative (*ḥujja*). The significance of the imam's role as an epistemic intermediary and teacher was also emphasized in Fatimid literature. For example, Ḥamīd al-Dīn Kirmānī (d. 412/1021) discussed the necessity for instruction due to the imperfection of the human soul and used the term along with divine inspiration (*ta'yīd*). He also maintained that ultimate actualization of the potential of the human soul is only possible through the 'instruction' (*taʿlīm*) of 'the pos-

1 Ṭūsī, *Contemplation and Action*, pp. 26–29.

sessors of divine inspiration' (*al-mu'ayyadīn*).[1] Ṭūsī, in his formulation of *taʿlīm* as the cause of actualizing the potential of the soul, argues along the same lines as Kirmānī. For Ṭūsī, 'without the instruction of a teacher, and the bringing into perfection by an agent of perfection, the attainment of truth is not possible.'[2] In another treatise that he wrote in collaboration with the Ismaʿili poet Ḥaṣan-i Maḥmūd, Ṭūsī presents a hierarchical division of knowledge with instructional knowledge being one level below the inspirational.[3] Below instructional knowledge is speculative knowledge, which is attained by philosophers. This knowledge is not divinely granted as in the case of inspirational knowledge (*ʿilm-i ta'yīdī*). Philosophical knowledge is discursive in that it involves the thought process. As a philosopher himself, Ṭūsī does not denounce discursive knowledge but simply ranks it lower than inspirational and instructional knowledge. There is strong evidence that in his philosophical writings Ṭūsī's awareness of the limit of human reason influenced his approach to those philosophical positions he finds in contradiction with what he deems to be the teachings of the Prophet or the imams. Yet, Ṭūsī's overall intellectual career also proves that he always regarded the activity of the human intellect through philosophy as an essential stepping-stone for understanding the meaning of religious beliefs and practices. A telling example is to be found in his *Tajrīd al-iʿtiqād* (The Summa of the Dogma), which is the first of his treatises on Twelver philosophical

1 Ḥamīd al-Dīn Kirmānī, *Rāḥat al-ʿaql*, eds., Kāmil Ḥusayn and Muḥammad Muṣṭafā Ḥilmī, Cairo: Dār al-Fikr al-ʿArabī, 1953, p. 304.
2 Ṭūsī, *Contemplation and Action*, p. 30.
3 Ṭūsī, *Rawḍa-yi taslīm*, ed. and trans. S. J. Badakhchani as *Paradise of Submission: A Medieval Treatise on Ismaili Thought*, London: I. B. Tauris in association with the Institute of Ismaili Studies, 2005, pp. 49–50.

theology. It is impossible to understand and appreciate this treatise without a significant command of Islamic philosophy. This is also true of Ṭūsī's approach to Ismaʿili doctrines of faith. While Ṭūsī argues that one learns pivotal doctrines of faith such as divine unity (*tawḥīd*) and creation through divine decree (*amr*) via the instruction of those who possess inspirational knowledge, he explains them by using conceptual tools borrowed from Greek and Muslim philosophers. Ṭūsī continued to rely on theoretical wisdom as formulated by his philosophical predecessors in almost all his works. The most obvious example of this methodological predilection is his reliance on reason and logic even in his theological works and here he was responsible for establishing a strong tradition of philosophical theology in Shiʿism that has been pursued to this day.

Wrestling with the Master's Critics

Although Ṭūsī was influenced by several intellectual traditions, he was mainly indebted to Ibn Sīnā for the general framework of his philosophical thought. His intellectual dedication to Ibn Sīnā was particularly visible in his attempts to defend the master in the face of criticisms by theologians. Ṭūsī's magnificent commentary on Ibn Sīnā's *al-Ishārāt wa'l-tanbīhāt* (The Pointers and Reminders), which he wrote during the period of his life among the Ismaʿilis, and *Talkhīṣ al-muḥaṣṣal* (A Summary of the Compendium), which he wrote later in his life, are both responses to the critiques of philosophy made by the famous Ashʿarī theologian Fakhr al-Dīn Rāzī (d. 606/1209), who states in a poem, 'In front of my writings Bū ʿAlī [Ibn Sīnā] would bend to prostrate/ I find Greek philosophy a kind of delirium.'[1]

1 Nasrollah Pourjavady, *Daw mujaddid: Muḥammad Ghazālī wa-Fakhr-i Rāzī*, Tehran: Markaz-i Nashr-i Dānishgāhī, 2003, p. 564.

Fakhr al-Dīn Rāzī's criticism of Ibn Sīnā's ideas is a continuation of the critique of some philosophical ideas started by Abū Ḥāmid Ghazālī (d. 505/1111) in his *Tahāfut al-falāsifa* (Incoherence of Philosophers). Both writers are considered defenders of Ashʿarī theology, which prioritizes what are deemed to be religious truths over rationalistic premises. From the formative age of Islamic intellectual history, Ashʿarism assumed the defence of religious dogma against the rationalism of the first school of Islamic theology (*kalām*), the Muʿtazila, and then against philosophy. However, this conflict should not be exaggerated to the point of oversimplifying some genuine intellectual critiques such as those by Fakhr al-Dīn Rāzī. For example, it has been claimed that in *al-Muḥassal*, when Rāzī addressed philosophical matters and used logical tools, his motive was to refute the authenticity and value of philosophy as such.[1] Such claims do not do justice to the sophisticated character of Rāzī's critiques, a fact that seems to have been appreciated by Ṭūsī himself.

It would be simplistic to reduce the intellectual encounter between Ṭūsī and Fakhr al-Dīn Rāzī to a mere conflict between Ashʿarism and Peripatetic philosophy. Rather than being torn apart between faith and reason, Islamic intellectual discourses have benefited from conversations. Whether or not one agrees with Rāzī in his critique of Ibn Sīnā, the depth and philosophical precision of some of his criticisms should not be underestimated just because he was a defender of Ashʿarism. According to Robert Wisnovsky, Rāzī's writings on the philosophy of Ibn Sīnā were a transition from partial commentaries on Ibn Sīnā to a comprehensive and systematic critical study of his work, and these writings

1 Ghulām Ḥusayn Ibrāhīmī Dīnānī, *Naṣīr al-Dīn Ṭūsī faylasūf-i guftigū*, Tehran: Hermes, 2007, pp. 216–217.

served as a model for later commentators.[1] He also correctly maintains that 'the survival and spread of Avicennism was due to both of them [Rāzī and Ṭūsī], not to Ṭūsī alone.'[2] Furthermore, in his later works on philosophical theology, Ṭūsī was inspired by Rāzī, especially by his famous *Mabāḥith al-mashriqiyya* (Oriental Investigations). In this respect, Ṭūsī's serious and respectful tone in his responses to Rāzī in the two above-mentioned works shows that he sees himself facing a mighty philosophical opponent. Looking at Fakhr al-Dīn Rāzī's works as a whole, one can say that he shared with Ṭūsī a mission to establish philosophical theology although the two had different theological positions. Despite their differences of opinion, Ṭūsī must have been inspired by Rāzī's attempt to discuss theological matters within a philosophical framework. The fact that Ṭūsī's commentary on Ibn Sīnā's *al-Ishārāt* became so popular with his contemporaries proves not only Ṭusī's academic influence during his lifetime, but also the significance of Rāzī's work too.[3]

Aside from his responses to Rāzī, Ṭūsī also responds to the criticisms of Ibn Sīnā made by ᶜAbd al-Karīm Shahristānī (d. 548/1153) in his *Muṣāriᶜ al-falāsifa* (Wrestling with the Philosophers). But Ṭūsī does not treat Shahristānī as respectfully as he does Fakhr al-Dīn Rāzī. In his rejoinder that he sarcastically calls *Muṣāriᶜ al-muṣāriᶜ* (Knocking Down of the Wrestler), Ṭūsī argues against Shahristānī demonstrat-

1 Robert Wisnovsky, 'Towards a Genealogy of Avicennism', *Oriens* vol. XIII, 2014, pp. 337–338.

2 Wisnovsky, 'Towards a Genealogy of Avicennism', p. 360.

3 On this subject, see Hasan Ansari, Preface to *Talkhīṣ al-Muḥaṣṣal* by Khwāja Naṣīr al-Dīn Ṭūsī, ed., Hasan Ansari, Tehran: Mīrāth-i Maktūb, 2016. On Rāzī's contributions to philosophical theology, see Aymen Shihadeh, 'From al-Ghazālī to al-Rāzī: 6th/12th Century Developments in Muslim Philosophical Theology', *Arabic Sciences and Philosophy*, vol. XV, 2005, pp. 141–179.

ing how some of his criticisms are based primarily on Isma'ili ideology rather than demonstrative logic. He indicates that Shahristānī's views are weak, groundless and based on wrong premises and dialectical arguments.[1]

Despite his attempts to defend Ibn Sīnā against his critics, Ṭūsī is not just an apologist for him and in several places he criticizes the master's views.

Crossing Boundaries

Ṭūsī did not establish a new philosophical system but he contributed to the formation of a fruitful conversation between different intellectual discourses that led to the redirection of Islamic philosophy towards a more synthetic methodology. Ṭūsī's intellectual orientation is towards crossing boundaries between Peripatetic, Illuminationist, Isma'ili, Sufi and theological discourses. For example, he has several treatises on metaphysical problems where philosophy and theology overlap; problems such as the division of existents (*qismat al-mawjūdāt*), the necessary being (*wājib al-wujūd*), providence and predestination (*al-qaḍā wa'l-qadar*), divine knowledge (*al-'ilm al-wājib*), the immaterial intellect (*al-'aql al-mufāraq*) and temporal origination of the bodily substance (*ḥudūth al-jism*). As mentioned above, his main treatise on Twelver theology, *Tajrīd al-i'tiqād*, is written within a Peripatetic framework. Furthermore, Ṭūsī's writings on Isma'ili doctrines are replete with philosophical premises and so are his texts on Sufism. His synthetic method is most noticeable in his writings on ethics and politics, which are equally dependent on Aristotle and the Qur'an.

One of Ṭūsī's earliest philosophical works is his commentary on Ibn Sīnā's *al-Ishārāt wa'l-tanbīhāt* (*Sharḥ al-Ishārāt*

1 Ṭūsī, *Muṣāri' al-muṣāri'*, ed. Shaykh Ḥassan al-Mu'izzī, Qom: Maktabat al-Manshūrāt Ayatollah al-Mar'ashī al-Najafī, 1985, p. 4.

wa'l-tanbīhāt), which he wrote at the request of Shihāb al-Dīn, the Ismaʿili chief of Quhistān. He spent many years writing this commentary and it still remains one of the main sources for understanding the intricacies of Ibn Sīnā's last philosophical work. This commentary is famous for its defence of Ibn Sīnā against the criticisms made by Fakhr al-Dīn Rāzī; this explains Ṭūsī's intentional avoidance of a critical approach to Ibn Sīnā except for a few instances where he finds criticism indispensable. Furthermore, by calling Ibn Sīnā 'divinely inspired' (*al-mu'ayyad*),[1] an Ismaʿili honorific title for those with access to certitude through God's assistance, Ṭūsī leaves little room for harsh criticism of him. While he would not place Ibn Sīnā at the same level with the Ismaʿili imam and his representative, by calling him '*mu'ayyad*' he is implying a divine source for his knowledge, which in Peripatetic context would be the agent intellect (*al-ʿaql al-faʿʿāl*), the immaterial source of intelligibles (*maʿqūlāt*) to which the human soul must resort for true knowledge.

Although Ṭūsī's commentary on Ibn Sīnā's work focuses on elucidating and defending the ideas of Ibn Sīnā, both in this work and in his other title *Tajrīd al-iʿtiqād*, he does depart from his master on a number of issues most important of which is divine knowledge, and the unity of the knower (*al-ʿāqil*, i.e., the subject of intellective knowledge) and the known (*al-maʿqūl*, i.e., the object of intellective knowledge).

God Knows All

In *al-Ishārāt*, Ibn Sīnā argues that 'Necessary Being' (*wājib al-wujūd*), or God, has knowledge of Himself through His Essence without any mediation and His knowledge of eve-

1 Ṭūsī, *Sharḥ al-Ishārāt wa'l-tanbīhāt*, ed. Sulayman Dunya, Cairo: Dār al-Maʿārif, 1960, vol. 1, p. 111.

rything other than Himself occurs because He is their cause or the principle of their existence. He also argues that divine knowledge is the noblest form of knowledge both with respect to the perceiver (*mudrik*) and the perceived (*mudrak*).[1] In elucidating Ibn Sīnā's position on the nobility of God's knowledge as the perceiver, Ṭūsī differentiates between active perception (*al-idrāk al-fiʿlī*) and passive perception (*al-idrāk al-infiʿālī*). In active perception, perceiving follows on from the bestowal of existence on the perceived, i.e., the object of God's perception. Here, divine knowledge is active—knowledge of the cause implies knowledge of the effect in its very essence or quiddity (*māhiyya*), as opposed to knowledge of the effect, which only implies knowledge of the existence of the cause rather than knowledge of its essence. In this regard, God's knowledge of Himself as the cause of all that is created by Him implies His perfect knowledge of their essences. With regard to God's knowledge of the perceived, it is the most noble knowledge because the objects of this knowledge are immaterial and universal, namely the intelligible substances (*al-jawāhir al-ʿaqliyya*).[2]

Ibn Sīnā goes on to mention a possible objection to the above argument, and his reply to it prompts Ṭūsī to argue against the master and to establish his own position on the relation between the subject and object of divine knowledge. According to Ibn Sīnā, while the intelligibles (*maʿqūlāt*) are not unified with the subject of knowledge, in this case God, or with each other, this does not imply multiplicity at the level of the divine Essence because the multiplicity of the intelligibles is posterior to and outside of God's knowledge of Himself as one simple reality. Here he uses the Qur'anic and Sufi term 'names' (*asmā'*) and

1 Ṭūsī, *Sharḥ al-Ishārāt wa'l-tanbīhāt*, vol. III, pp. 278–279.
2 Ibid., pp. 279–280.

says that 'multiplicity (*kathra*) of names has no impact on the unity (*waḥdāniyya*) of [God's] Essence.'[1] Ṭūsī clarifies this idea in accordance with his explicative method. He explains the concept of posteriority (*ta'akhkhur*) in terms of the causal relation between the divine Essence and the intelligibles: intelligibles are caused by God and are dependent on him; they are 'effects' and in their existence are 'posterior' to His Essence. Therefore, their multiplicity does not imply multiplicity at the level of the divine Essence.

Yet, Ṭūsī is not happy with this answer and reluctantly starts a line of argument contrary to his promise at the beginning of the *Sharḥ* not to take a stand against Ibn Sīnā. Here his main target is Ibn Sīnā's premise of the impossibility of unity between the subject and object of knowledge. While maintaining Ibn Sīnā's causal relation between subject and object, Ṭūsī uses it as a premise to prove the unity in God of subject and object of knowledge. His argument is premised on the active nature of divine knowledge as the cause of the objects of divine knowledge. Inspired by Shihāb al-Dīn Suhrawardī's formulation of knowledge by presence, Ṭūsī employs the term 'procession' (*ṣudūr*) and explains:

> ... Just as the intellector (*al-ʿāqil*) would not need any noetic form (*ṣūra*) but the form [i.e. reality] of its own self, which makes it what it is, in order to perceive itself for itself (*li dhātih*), it would also not need a form apart from the very form [i.e. reality] that proceeds (*yuṣdar*) from it to mediate its perception of that thing. Consider yourself as you conceive of (*tataṣawwar*) or summon (*tastaḥḍir*) a form which is generated by

1 Ibid., pp. 281–285.

> you. Although in doing this something other than you [i.e. the form] is involved, yet your knowledge of that form is not through another form [that represents it].[1]

Ṭūsī uses the above analogy of self-knowledge to prove that the very existence of the first effect (*al-maʿlūl al-awwal*) is God's knowledge of it and not any mediating form. To put it in Suhrawardī's terms (though his name does not appear in this context), God's knowledge of the first effect is knowledge by presence. The distinction of knowledge into knowledge by presence (*al-ʿilm al-ḥuḍūrī*) and knowledge by correspondence (*al-ʿilm al-ḥuṣūlī*) was already established by Ibn Sīnā. But, for Ibn Sīnā, the only example of knowledge by presence is self-knowledge while all other kinds of knowledge depend on noetic forms including divine knowledge of the world. Conversely, for Suhrawardī, all kinds of knowledge, both human and divine, are due to the immediate presence of the object of knowledge to the subject, that is, without the intermediary of noetic forms. He compares knowledge to vision and argues that God's knowledge and vision are one and 'nothing veils it from anything' in the heavens or the earth, alluding to the verse in the Qur'an that 'not the weight of an atom in the heavens or the earth escapes Him (Q. xxxiv.3).'[2] Thus, Ṭūsī follows Suhrawardī in taking a different path from that of Ibn Sīnā to prove that divine knowledge of multiple intelligibles does not imply multiplicity in the divine Essence. There is also a corollary to this conclusion. God's knowledge extends to both universals and particulars because every existent thing owes its existence to

1 Ibid., p. 283.
2 Shihāb al-Dīn Suhrawardī, *The Philosophy of Illumination*, eds. and trans. John Walbridge and Hossein Ziai, Provo, UT: Brigham Young University Press, 1999, p. 105.

God and by the same token they are present to God immediately in their realities (*bi-aʿyānihā*) rather than by way of mediation through noetic forms. To reinforce his argument, which again is similar to that of Suhrawardī, Ṭūsī cites the verse above and ends the section with a tone of confidence and gratitude for the blessing of awareness of the reality of God's knowledge.[1] Thirty years later in his *Tajrīd al-iʿtiqād*, Ṭūsī repeats the same argument about God's knowledge in a very concise manner as is the style of the treatise.[2] But his commentator, Ḥillī, expounds on the argument based on Ṭūsī's commentary on *al-Ishārāt* and refers the reader to the latter work. According to Ḥillī's commentary, Ṭūsī offers three modes of argument; the first he attributes to theologians and the last two to philosophers. After defining these modes of arguments, he gives his preference for the last one, which he believes demonstrates God's knowledge of both universals and particulars based on the causal relationship between God and the world:

> The last of the three arguments for God's knowledge argues for the extension of His knowledge to all that is known (*kullu maʿlumin*). It is premised on the fact that every existent thing beside God is contingent and every contingent is from Him, so He has knowledge of it whether it is a universal or a particular, whether it is a thing that sustains itself or is an accident of another thing, whether it is a thing that exists in the real world or is a concept in the mind since the mental forms of contingents

1 Ṭūsī, *Sharḥ al-Ishārāt wa'l-tanbīhāt*, vol. III, p. 285.

2 Muḥammad al-Muṭahhar al-Ḥillī, *Kashf al-murād fī sharḥ Tajrīd al-iʿtiqād*, ed. Ḥasan Ḥasanzāda Āmulī, Qom: Mu'assasa-i Nashr-i Islāmī, 1433 A.H., pp. 262–265.

> also come from Him, and whether or not it is the mental form of an existent thing or of a contingent that does not exist because nothing from the contingents or impossible things escapes His knowledge. This is a firm and noble demonstration.[1]

Ṭūsī's understanding of divine knowledge in terms of knowledge by presence is not solely dependent on Suhrawardī's thought but can also be connected to the Ismaʿili doctrine of the divine decree (*amr*), which is pivotal to Ṭūsī's Ismaʿili cosmology. It has been argued that Ṭūsī, especially in his autobiography, *Sayr wa-sulūk*, 'appears to be using Aristotle as interpreted by Avicenna [Ibn Sīnā] and Suhrawardī combined to prove the superiority of the presential knowledge of the divine *amr*.'[2] To clearly understand what is meant by the divine decree and its place in Ṭūsī's philosophy/theology is essential to a comprehensive interpretation of his work. A discussion of this subject in the next section will lead us to his philosophy of creation and cosmology. Moreover, his famous critique of the philosophers' doctrine of 'from the one (*wāḥid*) proceeds only one' appears in this context.

God is not the First Cause

Ibn Sīnā—and before him Abū Naṣr Fārābī (d. 339/950)—explains the causal connection between God and the world within a Neoplatonic framework of 'procession' (*ṣudūr*) that can be described as a kind of radiation or diffusion. While Fārābī's conception of God can be seen to be more similar to Aristotle's first cause as an eternal, self-contem-

1 Ḥillī, *Kashf al-murād*, p. 263.
2 Landolt, 'Khwājah Naṣīr al-Dīn al-Ṭūsī, Ismaʿīlism and Ishrāqī Philosophy', p. 21.

plating intellect, Ibn Sīnā systematically uses an existential language to describe God as the necessary being (*wājib al-wujūd*) on whose existence everything else in creation depends. Thus, in themselves, all things are contingent and incapable of reaching the level of existence unless existentiated by the necessary being or God. Ibn Sīnā's point of departure is, of course, Fārābī's view that the existence of God is 'unadulterated by non-existence [and] can in no way have existence potentially, and there is no possibility that it should not exist.'[1] Despite the differences in the details of their cosmologies, Fārābī and Ibn Sīnā agree on the metaphysical simplicity (*basāṭa*) of the first cause of the universe and affirm that it is one simple reality, and that this first cause or God brings forth via procession only one thing other than Himself.

Although the procession or emanation narrative was later criticized by the Andalusian philosopher Ibn Rushd (d. 595/1198) in favour of the Aristotelian cosmic paradigm, almost all major Muslim philosophers in the eastern lands of the Islamic world continued to adhere to the Avicennan procession theory of creation. The only other alternative to the idea of procession from God comes from the Persian school of Isma^cilism, most prominently Abū Ya^cqūb Sijistānī (d. after 360/971). Sijistānī maintains procession, yet, he refuses to ascribe it to God. In accordance with his negative theology, Sijistānī places God above existence and non-existence.[2] God is not even the first cause and we cannot say that anything proceeds from God. We can only

1 Abū Naṣr Fārābī, *Mabādi' ārā' ahl al-madīna al-fāḍila*, trans. Richard Walzer as *On the Perfect State*, Oxford: Clarendon Press, 1982, p. 57.
2 Abū Ya^cqūb Sijistānī, *Kashf al-mahjūb*, trans. Henry Corbin as *Le Dévoilement des choses cachées: Recherches de philosophie ismaélienne*, Lagrasse: Édition Verdier, 1988, p. 44.

describe God using negative language, that is, what God is not. For example, we can say that 'God is not non-existent.' To keep God outside the process of creation, Sijistānī posits an intermediary that he refers to by the Qur'anic term 'decree' (*amr*).[1] The decree, being the Word of God, brings into existence the universal intellect by the 'act of transcendent innovation' (*ibdāʿ*). Although the Fatimid Ismaʿili thinker Ḥamīd al-Dīn Kirmānī argued extensively against the intermediary state of the decree (*amr*),[2] most Ismaʿili figures after him such as Mu'ayyad fi'l-Dīn Shīrāzī (d. 470/1078) and Nāṣir-i Khusraw (d. after 469/1077) still followed Sijistānī. Ṭūsī too belongs to the Sijistānī camp with regard to the intermediary status of *amr*, but his terminology does not match perfectly with Sijistānī's. For Sijistānī, transcendent innovation is the primordial act of the divine decree.[3] The universal intellect is transcendentally innovated (*mubdaʿ*) and the creation of this universal intellect is attributed to the decree rather than to God, who is beyond the attribute of creativeness.

In contrast to Sijistānī, who does not use the term 'first cause' in reference to the divine decree as the act of transcendent innovation (*ibdāʿ*), Ṭūsī, in *Sayr wa-sulūk*, states that the first cause is the divine decree or *amr*. He argues that causality implies plurality and God is unity without plurality; therefore, God is not the first cause:

> ...Where there is [a concatenation] of cause
> and effect, there is no escape from plurality,

1 Q. II.117. *The Qur'an*, trans. M. A. S. Abdel Haleem, Oxford: Oxford University Press, 2016, p. 19.

2 See Ḥamīd al-Dīn Kirmānī, '*al-Risāla al-mawsūma bi'l-muḍī'a fi'l-amr wa'l-āmir wa'l-ma'mūr*', in Muṣṭafā Ghālib, ed. *Majmūʿat rasā'il al-Kirmānī*, Beirut: al-Mu'assasa al-Jāmiʿiyya li'l-Dirāsāt wa'l-Nashr wa'l-Tawzīʿ, 1983, pp. 113–133.

3 Sijistānī, *Kashf al-maḥjūb*, p. 36.

> but plurality cannot be allowed for the first origin of existents, since plurality cannot exist without unity. Such being the case, the True One—may His name be exalted—cannot insofar as He is the first origin, be attributed with cause or effect...From this, it becomes clear that in the terminology of philosophers, it is an error to speak of the first cause in relation to God, but it is correct to apply it to His command which is the source of all existence.[1]

Ṭūsī proceeds to ascribe several characteristics to the divine decree. First, he characterizes it as the intermediary of creation due to its possessing two facets, one towards the unity of the divine Essence and the other towards the multiplicity of the created or contingent world beginning with the universal intellect (*ʿaql-i kullī*). Second, due to these two facets, one can say that the decree is not additional to the divine Essence 'in so far as He is He...but from the point of view where [the decree] is the cause of an effect, it is something additional.'[2] Third, the decree is not only the origin of all existents, but also the point of return for all existents; it is both the efficient cause and the final end of all creation. Fourth, the decree has the noblest form of knowledge because it knows God through God and as a result it is the origin of 'all forms of knowledge and perfections [that] pour forth from it upon the intellects and souls.'[3] This point in particular has been the focus of study of the influence of Ismaʿili philosophy on Ṭūsī's position on divine knowledge and its characterization as presential (*ḥuḍūrī*), and it illus-

1 Ṭūsī, *Contemplation and Action*, pp. 37 & 38.
2 Ibid., p. 37.
3 Ibid., p. 41.

trates that Suhrawardī was not the only influence here.[1] Fifth, the decree is connected to the sensible world through the locus of its manifestation (*maẓhar*) who is 'an individual human being who appears to be like other human beings [one who] is born, grows old and succeeds to the one before him in a continuous line so that it [the decree] will be preserved in perpetuity [among mankind].'[2]

Thus, Ṭūsī's discourse on the decree is different from Sijistānī's in two respects. First, he refers to it as the first cause (*ʿillat-i ūlā*) and considers it additional to the divine Essence at the level of its causal facet. The term 'first cause' appears both in *Sayr wa-sulūk* and in *Rawḍa-yi taslīm*.[3] Second, he ascribes to the decree a level of manifestation in the sensible world, namely, the Ismaʿili imam. Regarding the first difference, Ṭūsī's use of the term 'causality' can be understood in light of his dedication to Ibn Sīnā's conceptual framework, which is the background of all his philosophical and theological writings. According to Ṭūsī, all the attributes of the first cause in philosophy can be ascribed to the decree.[4] For example, he explains as procession (*ṣudūr*) the causal relation between the decree and the universal intellect, which is transcendent innovation (*ibdāʿ*) in Ismaʿili terms. He describes the decree as 'one pure light, one uncontaminated emanation (*fayḍ*), one bounty (*jūd*), and one generosity (*sakhā'*).'[5] But Sijistānī's application of 'procession', which he refers to as '*inbiʿāth*', is limited to the level of the universal soul, which is said to proceed from

1 See Landolt, 'Khwājah Naṣīr al-Dīn al-Ṭūsī, Ismaʿīlism and Ishrāqī Philosophy'.
2 Ṭūsī, *Contemplation and Action*, p. 41.
3 Ṭūsī, *Paradise of Submission*, p. 21.
4 Ṭūsī, *Contemplation and Action*, p. 38.
5 Ṭūsī, *Paradise of Submission*, p. 20.

the intellect. In Sijistānī's philosophy, the main difference between *ibdāʿ* and *inbiʿāth* is that the former is best understood as creation out of nothing while the latter is similar to Neoplatonic emanation of one entity from another.[1] There is a possibility that Ṭūsī is using the term 'procession' figuratively, but due to the sensitivity of such terminology in Ismaʿili texts, his divergence from Sijistānī's narrative must not be underestimated.

In his discourse on creation, Ṭūsī criticizes the inferences made by philosophers from the axiom 'from the one proceeds only one'; this axiom is one of the premises based on which philosophers argue for the existence of the intellects. His critique of their position is especially important as a link between his Ismaʿili writings and those of his later works, that do not include Ismaʿili ideas. In his commentary on Ibn Sīnā's *al-Ishārāt wa'l-tanbīhāt*, Ṭūsī discusses this axiom in the section on the existence of the intellects and the relation of the first intellect to necessary being (*wājib al-wujūd*), or God. According to Ibn Sīnā, procession of multiple things implies multiplicity of conceptual considerations (*iʿtibārāt*) and modes (*jihāt*) in the cause. As the necessary being is simple (*basīṭ*) in every respect, only one thing can proceed from it. In his commentary, Ṭūsī simply elucidates Ibn Sīnā's position and highlights the difference between the first cause and its effects in terms of the simplicity of the former and the existence of multiple aspects in the latter. He explains that while the first cause is pure of multiplicity, it is the origin of all multiplicity in the world through the intermediary (*wisāṭa*) of its effects. For example, if A is the first cause and B is the first effect

1 See Paul E. Walker, *Early Philosophical Shiism: The Ismaili Neoplatonism of Abū Yaʿqūb al-Sijistānī*, Cambridge: Cambridge University Press, 1993, pp. 81–86.

from which proceeds C, then we can infer that C proceeds from A through the intermediary of B. The line of processions can continue ad infinitum but we can always trace all the proceeded multiplicity back to the first cause while the simplicity of the first cause is not touched.[1] He also identifies six conceptual considerations (*iʿtibārāt*) of multiplicity in the first effect, that is, in the first intellect: existence (*wujūd*), quiddity (*māhiyya/huwiyya*), contingency (*imkān*), necessitation (*wujūb*) [by the first cause], self-intellection (*taʿaqqul li'l-dhāt*) and intellection of the origin (*taʿaqqul li'l-mabdaʾ*).[2] These multiple considerations in the first effect, which will be multiplied further in the next effects, guarantee the existence of multiplicity in the world while the first cause is pure and simple with none of the multiple considerations.

In his criticism of the philosophers' arguments for the existence of the intellects, it is important to note that Ṭūsī does not set forth a conclusive argument against the intellects; all he tries to show is that the philosophers' arguments for their existence are not cogent. Yet, in the *Tajrīd*, Ṭūsī does not present any argument as to why the axiom 'from the one proceeds only one' does not imply the procession of the first intellect from God. He limits himself to saying that considering the free agency of God, this axiom is not valid.[3] Here, Ṭūsī takes it for granted that the reader remembers his argument against the philosophers' inference from his earlier works such as *Fuṣūl al-ʿaqā'id* (Divisions of the Creeds). Thus in the *Tajrīd*, Ṭūsī criticizes the axiom mainly in the context of proving free agency (*ikhtīyār*) for God alone. He maintains that due to their belief in this axiom, philosophers have considered God as a necessary cause rather than a free

1 Ṭūsī, *Sharḥ al-Ishārāt wa'l-tanbīhāt*, vol. III, pp. 216–218.
2 Ibid., p. 219.
3 Ḥillī, *Kashf al-murād*, p. 155.

agent who creates at will. So, he tries to demonstrate that the axiom is problematic and must be abandoned with respect to God's agency. According to him, the six multiple aspects of the first intellect, that is, existence, quiddity, contingency, necessitation [by the first cause], self-intellection and intellection of the origin, are not realities that can be sources of multiplicity. If these aspects were real, they would need a cause. If we assume God to be the cause of these multiple realities, then God would not be simple and this would contradict what the philosophers believe. On the other hand, if they were real and God was not their cause, then they would have to have another cause and this is impossible because that would imply multiple Gods. Ṭūsī concludes that the multiple aspects of the first intellect are not real, as only real things can have real effects.[1] It seems that in his commentary on one of Ṭūsī's last writings, *Qawāʿid al-fawā'id*, Ḥillī explains the author's criticism of the axiom based on his knowledge of *Fuṣūl al-ʿaqā'id*. This is because in the former, Ṭūsī does not argue based on the inauthenticity of the six multiple aspects of the first intellect, while Ḥillī mentions the six aspects and argues that three of them, 'contingency, necessitation, and intellection', are not realities and therefore cannot have any effects in the real world, that is, the existence of the next beings after the first intellect.[2]

Overall, Ṭūsī argues that philosophers have been wrong in deducing the procession of the first intellect from God on the basis of the axiom 'from the one proceeds only one'.

1 Ṭūsī, *Fuṣūl al-ʿaqā'id*, cited in Gholāmreza Mīnāgar, 'Nigāhī bi naw'āwarīhā-yi falsafī wa-kalāmī-ya Khwājah Naṣīr al-Dīn Ṭūsī', *Faṣlnāma-yi ḥikmat wa-falsafa*, vol. 1, 2010, p. 134.

2 Muḥammad al-Muṭahhar al-Ḥillī, *Kashf al-fawā'id fī sharḥ Qawāʿid al-ʿaqā'id*, ed. Ḥasan al-Makkī al-ʿĀmilī, Beirut: Dār al-Ṣafwa, 1993, p. 264.

However, in the works mentioned above it is not exactly clear what he proposes as an alternative to the procession of the first intellect from God, and his doctrine of God as a free agent is simply put forth as a theological posit. It is only in his Ismaʿili writings that Ṭūsī presents an alternative to the necessary procession from God and argues for the necessity of an intermediary between God and the first (or universal) intellect. In *Sayr wa-sulūk*, after explaining the axiom in a very similar manner to his explanation in the commentary on *al-Ishārāt*, Ṭūsī proceeds to argue that if the procession of two entities requires the existence of two aspects (*thubūt-i daw iʿtibār*), then the procession of one entity would require the existence of one aspect (*thubūt-i yak iʿtibār*) which is conceptually differentiated from God. According to Ṭūsī, this one aspect, namely, the divine decree, which is a reality capable of causing another entity, is only recognized by the Ismaʿilis.[1]

In *Rawḍa-i taslīm*, Ṭūsī continues to argue for the divine decree as the intermediary of creation and he again criticizes the axiom of 'from the one proceeds only one'. Yet, here his criticism is of the application of the axiom rather than the axiom itself, and he questions the philosophers' assumption of direct procession from God. He criticizes the philosophers' application of the axiom to God in that it contradicts divine unity. Yet, in this treatise, Ṭūsī also frames the issue of creation as a dilemma for theoretical reason and maintains the axiom as valid from certain perspectives. Regarding the dilemma of creation for the faculty of reason, he explains that for reason there are absurd consequents for both affirming the possibility of emergence of things from God and denying this. Affirming the possibility would

1 Ṭūsī, *Contemplation and Action*, p. 36.

imply multiplicity in God and denying it would imply the unreality of creation especially as the object of God's knowledge. It is due to this dilemma that an intermediary is posited, namely, the divine decree. But the decree can only be spoken of through metaphors such as 'illumination' and 'absolute grace' and every creature understands creation according to 'the existential rank that it has received from His exalted command.'[1] It is with respect to this existential perspectivism that Ṭūsī re-establishes a place for the axiom in question. He says that the first intellect could say 'from the one can proceed only one' with respect to its own knowledge and vision of the oneness of the decree, and the universal soul (which proceeds from the first intellect but through its intermediary also governs and organizes the bodily world) would say that 'from the one can only proceed one, and [from another aspect] many.'[2] Ṭūsī's line of argument in this treatise and his perspectival usage of the axiom proves that he acknowledges different contexts for discussing creation and that his criticism of the axiom is not related to its content but to its rigid application to God by philosophers. Yet there is one manner of speaking about creation that he prohibits in his Ismaʿili texts, that is, to speak of God as the first cause. Any causation or procession starts from one aspect of God, that is, his decree or word.

Finally, in Ṭūsī's discussion of the decree there is his elaboration on the application of this doctrine to the status of the imam. Here, he again differs from the Ismaʿili philosopher Sijistānī. Generally speaking, while Sijistānī has an elaborate theory of prophecy, the imamate has an insignificant place in his works. In contrast, Ṭūsī's occupation with the imamate is very intense and he considers the imam as the

1 Ṭūsī, *Paradise of Submission*, pp. 27–28.
2 Ibid., p. 29.

manifestation of the divine decree in the sensible world. It has been stated that Ṭūsī's Ismaʿili imamology is informed by the Nizārī Ismaʿili emphasis on the role of the imam in the cyclical history of humanity.[1]

Creation and Time

The relation of time to creation is a common subject in both metaphysics and theology and is one of the most controversial issues in Islamic thought; it is an area in which theologians and philosophers have clashed. For example, theologians objected to the arguments for the eternity of the world made by Fārābī and Ibn Sīnā. Ibn Sīnā's position, which is called 'origination in essence' (*al-ḥudūth al-dhātī*), is famously rivalled by the theologian's belief in the 'temporal origination of the world' (*al-ḥudūth al-zamānī*). In his commentary on Ibn Sīnā's *al-Ishārāt*, Ṭūsī explains the two positions as follows: For theologians (*mutakallimūn*), the world's need for a cause or agent (*fāʿil*) is explained on the basis of temporal origination. They mostly argue that the cause brought a previously non-existent world into existence. In contrast, for philosophers the world needed a cause not due to its previous non-existence, but because contingency (*imkān*) is the essential aspect of everything but the first cause. Ṭūsī refutes the theological position in defence of Ibn Sīnā. He argues that although it seems that the theologians' position on temporal origination is premised on God as a free agent, the reverse is true: theologians deduce the necessity of a free agent from temporal origination. He also says that the philosophers' eternity of the world does not contradict a free agent and that they only argue that an eternal world must have been created by an

1 See Daftary, *The Ismāʿīlīs*, pp. 379–381.

eternal cause and that the creator's free agency (*ikhtiyār*) is not additional to the divine Essence.[1] This last remark is important evidence for the continuity between Ṭūsī's philosophical commentary and his later theological works in which he argues for the free agency of God in creation.

Ṭūsī's understanding of the nature of time remains the same in both his commentary on *al-Ishārāt* and in the *Tajrīd*. In both these works he relies on two key concepts to explain the nature of time—priority (*qabliyya*) and posteriority (*baʿdiyya*). For Ṭūsī, time is a fluid or unstable entity whose existence is manifest to us while its essence is hidden. The existence of time can be understood through the concepts of priority and posteriority. Yet priority and posteriority are only in the mind rather than being actual aspects of time. Therefore, the mystery of time consists in the fact that we understand time as a passage from a previous state or a 'priority' to one that follows it, namely, a 'posteriority'. But at the same time, we cannot conceive of priority and posteriority without a conception of time because priority and posteriority are only in the mind.[2] It is important to note that Ṭūsī's argument for temporal origination is limited to the physical world and his understanding of priority and posteriority is a premise to prove the temporal origination of the physical world. For Ṭūsī, time is conceived due to the expiration and renewal that are changes in the state of a substratum capable of changing, that is, the bodily substance (*jism*).[3] It is because of the expiration and renewal that we conceive of prior and posterior. So, for Ṭūsī, we cannot speak of time outside of the material zone.

Also in the *Tajrīd*, Ṭūsī tries to prove that the philosophers'

1 Ṭūsī, *Sharḥ al-Ishārāt wa'l-tanbīhāt*, vol. III, pp. 65–71.
2 Ibid., p. 72.
3 Ibid., p. 75.

arguments for the eternity of the world are based on their misunderstanding of priority and posteriority. He summarizes their arguments as follows: if the world was not eternal, the posteriority of an effect to a cause would either be due to some change or no change in the state of the cause. If we accept that some change took place, then what follows would be the absurd consequent that the sufficient cause was not a sufficient cause, that is, a reduction *ad absurdum*. If no change took place, then the choice to create at a particular moment in time rather than another would be a case of determination without a determinant (*tarjīḥ bi-lā murajjaḥ*), which is impossible.

Ṭūsī continues by saying that the sufficient cause of creation is eternal, while time comes into existence at the beginning of the origination of the bodily world. His objection to the philosophers' argument is that the two concepts of priority and posteriority exist only in the mind (*wahmī*). For him, before time comes into existence along with the body, there is no priority or posteriority, so the concern about a determinant for choosing one time over another is unreasonable. Time was not preceded by time, but it came into existence along with the origination of bodily substances.

In order to make his point clear, Ṭūsī needs to explain why time is inseparable from bodily substances. His argument is mainly based on his understanding of time in its relation to the natural state of bodies as finite spatial entities. According to him, the reason why bodies are finite temporal components is because they are necessarily characterized as either moving or not moving, and both motion and rest (*ḥaraka wa-sukūn*) are temporal. Every bodily entity is in a certain space (*makān*). If it stays in that space, we call it motionless, and when it leaves that space, we say that it moved. It is thus granted that every bodily substance is spatial and being spatial it either moves or rests. Now, both motion and rest are originated within time. When we say that a thing moved, we mean that it left one place for another. And when we say that a thing did not move, we mean that it stayed in the same place where it was previously. Therefore, both motion and rest are preceded by a previous state; this makes them originated because an eternal thing is not preceded by any prior state or thing. As priority and posteriority result from the mind's analysis of time, motion and rest are essentially temporal states and thus bodies are originated within time.[1] Ṭūsī's argument, therefore, ascribes temporal origination only to particular events and applies the concept only to the physical world because it consists of a chain of particular temporal events. Throughout he retains the important assumption that the world as a whole is only a consideration of the mind rather than an actual reality to which we can ascribe eternity or temporality.

To conclude the discussion of time and creation in Ṭūsī's writings, it is clear that with respect to metaphysical issues—and even in his theological works—Ṭūsī's preference is for logical demonstrations rather than theological arguments premised on conventional religious dogma.

The Human Soul, From Whence it Comes and Where it Goes

Studies of the soul (*nafs*) in mediaeval texts can be divided into metaphysical psychology and cognitive psychology. Metaphysical psychology addresses the soul's nature, origin, faculties and its relation to the body; it also includes the extent of the soul's dependence on the individual body and the question of its immortality after the death of the body. This last topic overlaps with eschatology, that is, the status

1 Ḥillī, *Kashf al-murād*, p. 150.

of the soul in the afterlife. For cognitive psychology, the primary question is the process of knowledge formation initiated by the soul's relationship with the external world, as well as any internal and external grounds and conditions for true knowledge. Some of the findings in the area of cognitive psychology are related to epistemology.

In Ṭūsī's philosophical Isma'ili and Twelver writings, he largely remains faithful to Ibn Sīnā's psychology. For example, he maintains the Peripatetic definition of the soul as 'the first perfection (*al-kamāl al-awwal*) of the natural organic body.'[1] This is the definition of the soul that includes the vegetative, animal and human souls, and which distinguishes the human soul from the other two through its possession of the faculty of rationality (*nuṭq*). In the *Tajrīd*, Ṭūsī disagrees with the Aristotelian idea where the soul is defined as the form of the organic body. For Ṭūsī, form is immanent (*ḥāll*) in matter while the human soul is not immanent in the body.[2] In addition, the human soul is not to be identified as the natural composition (*mizāj*) of the body. Rather it is the preserver and unifier of contrasting elements that make up the natural composition. Without an independent substance like the soul that can pull them together, the elements that constitute the bodily nature would be in conflict with each other and the body would disintegrate.[3] In *Rawḍa-yi taslīm,* Ṭūsī describes the human soul as 'a separate, nonmaterial (*mufāraq*) substance whose connection with the body is for the purpose of stimulating motion and alteration (*taḥrīk wa-taghyīr*).' The proof that Ṭūsī offers for the independence of the soul from the

1 Ṭūsī, *Sharḥ al-Ishārāt wa'l-tanbīhāt*, vol. II, p, 343; *Paradise of Submission*, p. 36; Ḥillī, *Kashf al-murād*, p. 160.
2 Ḥillī, *Kashf al-murād*, p. 161.
3 Ṭūsī, *Sharḥ al-Ishārāt wa'l-tanbīhāt*, vol. II, pp. 352–353; Ḥillī, *Kashf al-murād*, pp. 162–163.

natural composition of the body is the occurrence of 'voluntary motion in various directions' and 'perception'. As for voluntary motion, the natural composition of the body can only cause motion in the direction required by the majority of its components, or cause rest in a certain location required by these same components.[1] But the soul is independent of the natural composition of the body.

As for perception, the natural composition of the body cannot be the agent of perception due to the potential conflicts between the components. For example, in nature, fire and water cannot co-exist without one obliterating the other. Perception consists in the 'impression' of a subject by an object and this, as the example above shows, cannot happen between natural elements. In any form of perception, the perceiver and the perceived must both remain in existence.[2] Thus, for Ṭūsī, the soul is an immaterial substance and it governs the body, and a proof of its immateriality (*tajarrud*) can be found in Ibn Sīnā's thought experiment of the dangling man (*al-insān al-muʿallaq*). In this thought experiment, Ibn Sīnā shows that in the absence of all senses and contact with external objects, the hypothetical soul in the void would still be capable of perceiving its own existence, that is, self-awareness, which means it must be independent of the body.[3]

The classical argument for the immateriality of the soul is based on the concept of indivisibility (*ʿadam al-inqisām*): 1) anything material is divisible, 2) the soul is not divisible, 3) therefore, the soul is not material. Ṭūsī's arguments for the indivisibility of the soul again are based on Ibn Sīnā's arguments. According to Ṭūsī in the *Rawḍa*,

1 Ṭūsī, *Sharḥ al-Ishārāt wa'l-tanbīhāt*, vol. II, pp. 351–352.

2 Ibid., vol. II, p. 352; Ḥillī, *Kashf al-murād*, p. 162.

3 Ṭūsī, *Sharḥ al-Ishārāt wa'l-tanbīhāt*, vol. II, p. 344.

'if the human soul were divisible, it would be ignorant of something in one part [of the soul] and aware of the same thing in another part.'[1] And in the *Tajrīd*, he says that, as the subject of knowledge, the soul is indivisible because knowledge itself is indivisible.[2] For example, our knowledge of mathematics does not reside in one part of the soul and our knowledge of geography in another so that each part would be unaware of the other.

With all its immaterial simplicity, the soul still possesses different faculties (*quwā*). In Ibn Sīnā's division, the four faculties of the soul consist of: sense perception, imagination, estimation (namely a grasp of particular meanings, such as the fear of wolves in a sheep) and finally intellection. The first three are shared between humans and animals, while only human beings possess intellection. The faculty of intellection, or the rational soul (*al-nafs al-nāṭiqa*), is itself divided into several functional stages with regard to the acquisition of knowledge. It is due to the development and function of intellection that human beings are distinguished from each other intellectually.[3] Ṭūsī describes the levels of intellection as different in rank (*tarattub*) and excellence (*tafāḍul*). The development of the intellect via several stages, from its primary level of potentiality, 'the material intellect' (*al-ʿaql al-hayūlānī*), to the noble level of the 'acquired intellect' (*al-ʿaql al-mustafād*), which contains all the intelligibles, is described as an existential expansion of the soul.

But, in the beginning the human soul is a mere potenti-

1 Ṭūsī, *Paradise of Submission*, p. 35.

2 Ḥillī, *Kashf al-murād*, p. 164. The narrative that Ṭūsī uses to explain the evolution of the soul anticipates the later metaphysical psychology, most prominently that of the Safavid philosopher Mullā Ṣadrā Shīrāzī (d. 1045/1640).

3 Ṭūsī, *Paradise of Submission*, p. 37.

ality in the sense that it is not fully actualized in its 'soulness' or spirituality. In other words, it cannot be regarded as immaterial in the exact sense of the word. Ṭūsī explains that 'the soul's particular activity is to become, gradually and by degrees, an immaterial form (*ṣūrat-i mujarrad*).'[1] This can happen through knowledge, which I will discuss in the next section.

Human Knowledge and the Necessity for Instruction

In both his Ismaʿili and Twelver texts, Ṭūsī divides human knowledge into 'necessary/self-evident' (*ḍarūrī/badīhī*) and 'acquired/speculative' (*kasbī/naẓarī*) knowledge.[2] The division between the two forms of knowledge is based on the absence of the thought process (*fikr*) in the former and its requirement in the latter. Self-evident knowledge is based on truths and axioms that have already been proven, while speculative knowledge demands the mental effort to arrive at a conclusion. An example that Ṭūsī gives for self-evident knowledge is that, in an object, the whole is larger than its parts. His example for speculative knowledge is that one's existence is not due to one's own will, otherwise people, upon their coming into existence, would have given themselves all the possible perfections.[3]

As for speculative knowledge and its efficient cause, Ṭūsī's two texts, namely the *Rawḍa* and the *Tajrīd*, diverge over the necessity for instruction (*taʿlīm*) as the cause for speculative knowledge. In the *Rawḍa* (which is one of Ṭūsī's Ismaʿili works), Ṭūsī posits the necessity of an instructor who is in charge of actualizing the potential of the soul to gain knowledge. He considers knowledge as a perfection

1 Ibid., p. 36.
2 Ibid., p. 49; Ḥillī, *Kashf al-murād*, p. 217.
3 Ṭūsī, *Paradise of Submission*, 49.

that can be bestowed by someone who already possesses it and compares the process by analogy to the mover and the moved, a typical Aristotelian narrative of efficient causality.[1] The instructor is someone who has received divine knowledge directly, a kind of knowledge that in Isma^cili terminology is called 'inspirational' (*tayīdī*). This type of knowledge belongs to the imam and through him to his representative, namely, the *ḥujja*.

Yet, in the *Tajrīd*, Ṭūsī refutes the necessity for instruction as the efficient cause of speculative knowledge. Following Ibn Sīnā, who in turn follows a Neoplatonic reading of Aristotle, Ṭūsī believes in the active role of the 'agent intellect' (*al-ʿaql al-faʿʿāl*)—which is external to the human mind—in conferring intelligibles on the rational soul. He defines the agent intellect as 'an entity that contains all the intelligible forms, that is neither material nor psychological.'[2] The Peripatetic agent intellect is the tenth intellect in the hierarchy of intellective substances that proceed from each other and it is not connected with a particular manifestation in the sensible world. Ṭūsī does mention this agent intellect in his Ismaʿili writings. However, in the Ismaʿili texts, the agent intellect is another name for the universal intellect that is originated in eternity by the divine decree[3] and this universal intellect has a particular manifestation in the sensible world in the representative, or *ḥujja*, of the imam. The imam himself is the sensible manifestation of the divine decree.[4]

Ṭūsī argues that philosophy and revelation both prove the necessity for instruction by someone who has an immedi-

1 Ṭūsī, *Contemplation and Action*, pp. 29–30.
2 Ṭūsī, *Sharḥ al-Ishārāt wa'l-tanbīhāt*, vol. II, p. 397.
3 Ṭūsī, *Paradise of Submission*, p. 29.
4 Ṭūsī, *Contemplation and Action*, p. 41.

ate knowledge of truths. As for philosophy, Ṭūsī suggests a thesis from Ibn Sīnā's philosophy though he does not mention him by name in this context. This is Ibn Sīnā's thesis of 'the prophetic faculty' (*al-quwwa al-qudsiyya*),[1] which is differentiated from the discursive faculty due to the instantaneous (*dafʿī*) and effortless formation of certain knowledge for very few souls.[2] As for revelation, Ṭūsī associates it with the perspective of the followers of the exoteric (*ahl-i ẓāhir*) who follow 'the possessor of bestowed knowledge' (*ʿilm-i ladunnī*), who must be a prophet or an imam.[3] While both philosophy and revelation can be sources of true knowledge, 'those who cling to only the exoteric aspects of these two methods remain deprived of, and veiled from, the knowledge of it.'[4] In other words, it is the manner of receiving knowledge from the teacher that makes it either instructional (*taʿlīmī*) or inspirational (*ta'yīdī*). As Ṭūsī says:

> Approaching a teacher of comprehensive knowledge—if he teaches one in a systematic manner, relying on exoteric expressions explained and understood sequentially and gradually—it is called instruction (*taʿlīm*); but if [the knowledge] is given to one by esoteric means and received instantaneously, it is called divine inspiration (*ta'yīd*).[5]

As can be seen from this quotation, there is a difference between Ibn Sīnā's narrative of inspirational knowledge and Ṭūsī's. For Ibn Sīnā, the giver of such knowledge is the agent intellect itself, while for Ṭūsī the imam and his *ḥujja*

1 Ibid., p. 33.
2 Ṭūsī, *Sharḥ al-Ishārāt wa'l-tanbīhāt*, vol. II, pp. 394–395.
3 Ṭūsī, *Contemplation and Action*, p. 33.
4 Ibid., pp. 36–37.
5 Ṭūsī, *Paradise of Submission*, p. 50.

can play that role with regard to their followers. The *ḥujja* receives 'the outpouring of the imam's illuminations' (*fayḍ-i anwār-i tayīd-i imām*)[1] and in turn bestows it on those who seek his instruction.[2] The role of *ḥujja* is especially prominent during the concealment of a ruling imam. Here, Ṭūsī's contribution to the Nizārī doctrine of instruction and the role of *ḥujja* is considerable in that he frames it philosophically and strengthens it from within the wider conceptual framework of Peripatetic philosophy.

The Origin and the End of the Soul

Despite different interpretations of Aristotle's definition of the soul as 'form of the body' or 'perfection (*entelechy*) of the body', there is one definite way that most Muslim philosophers depart from Aristotle. They consider the human soul as separable from the body. Informed by the Arabic translation of Plotinus' *The Enneads*[3] as well as the pivotal doctrine of resurrection (*maʿād*) in Islam, Ibn Sīnā and his followers interpret Aristotle's definition of the soul-body relationship in a way to guarantee the soul's separability from the body after the death of the body.[4]

Yet, for Ibn Sīnā, the soul—despite its separability—does not precede the body in existence. He is opposed to the Platonic view of the pre-existence of the soul. In his *al-Shifāʾ*, Ibn Sīnā provides extensive arguments for

1 Ṭūsī, *Paradise of Submission*, p. 131.

2 For more on this subject see my *Knowledge and Power in the Philosophies of Ḥamīd al-Dīn Kirmānī and Mullā Ṣadrā Shīrāzī*, London: Palgrave-Macmillan, 2018, pp. 95–102.

3 See Peter Adamson, *The Arabic Plotinus: A Philosophical Study of the Theology of Aristotle*, London: Duckworth, 2002, pp. 50–54.

4 Ibn Sīnā, *Avicenna's De anima: Being the Psychological Part of Kitāb al-Shifaʾ*, ed. Fazlur Rahman. London: Oxford University Press, 1959, p. 227.

the origination (*ḥudūth*) of the soul along with the body.[1] The soul is given to the body by one of the 'immaterial causes' (*al-ʿilal al-mufāraqa*),[2] that is, by the agent intellect as the bestower of all substantial forms, once the body is ready for it. Different organic compositions receive their appropriate souls on the basis of their different capacities, hence the division of vegetative, animal and rational souls. In his commentary on Ibn Sīnā's *al-Ishārāt*, Ṭūsī expounds on Ibn Sīnā's origination of the soul by tracing the development of the human foetus. Relying on two concepts, perfection (*kamāl*) and reception (*qabūl*), he explains that as the foetus grows physically, it also grows in its capacity for receiving the vegetative (*nabātī*) and animal (*ḥayawānī*) souls that are the source of vegetative acts such as nutrition and animal acts such as motion. The final stage of perfection is the reception of the rational soul (*al-nafs al-nāṭiqa*) from which issue all the previous acts as well as rationality (*nuṭq*). The soul preserves the body and governs it until the death of the body. The three souls mentioned above are three stages of the same entity.[3]

In his *Tajrīd*, Ṭūsī argues against the pre-existence of the soul and says that to believe in its pre-existence would entail absurd consequents. Ṭūsī's argument goes as follows: if all souls were originally one soul, then this one soul would have to multiply into different souls once bodies came into existence. If it did not do so, then this would result in the absurd consequent where all human beings would possess the same soul and identical knowledge.[4]

In Ṭūsī's Ismaʿili texts, one would expect a different

1 Ibid., pp. 223–227.

2 Ibid., 233.

3 Ṭūsī, *Sharḥ al-Ishārāt wa'l-tanbīhāt*, vol. II, pp. 355–356.

4 Ḥillī, *Kashf al-murād*, p. 167–168.

characterization of the soul's beginning given the Platonic background of the Persian school of Ismaᶜili philosophy, most importantly that of Sijistānī.[1] But this is not the case. In the *Rawḍa*, which includes several sections on the soul, Ṭūsī argues that the soul is not 'pre-eternal' (*azalī*)[2] and describes it in the Aristotelian terms of the first perfection of the natural organic body.[3] In his *Āghāz wa-anjām* (Origin and Destination), which is heavily laden with Qur'anic language and references, he states the creation of humankind was out of nothing.[4] Thus, there seems to be no trace of the idea of the pre-existence of the human soul in Ṭūsī's Ismaᶜili writings.

What does distinguish Ṭūsī's Ismaᶜili writings from his other texts is their characterization of the afterlife for the soul. In a very innovative way, Ṭūsī relies on the power of imagination to describe the quality of the afterlife for the soul. Inspired by Suhrawardī, he maintains that the imaginative faculty of the human soul, which in this context he characterizes as a type of soul, i.e. the imaginal soul (*nafs-i khayālī*), has a face turned towards the world of sense perception and a face turned towards the intelligibles; it thus has the power to retain ideas even in the absence of the body and to 'become co-eternal with the eternity of the soul' after the death of the body:

> When the soul departs from the body, it

1 For a discussion of the soul in this school, see Paul E. Walker, 'The Universal Soul and the Particular Soul in Ismaᶜīlī Neoplatonism', in Parviz Morewedge, ed., *Neoplatonism and Islamic Thought*, Albany, NY: State University of New York Press, 1992, pp. 149–166.

2 Ṭūsī, *Paradise of Submission*, p. 34.

3 Ibid., p. 36.

4 Ṭūsī, *Āghāz wa-anjām*, trans. S. J. Badakhchani as *Origin and Destination*, in S. J. Badakhchani, ed., *Shiᶜi Interpretations of Islam: Three Treatises on Theology and Eschatology*, London: I. B. Tauris & the Institute of Ismaili Studies, 2010, p. 52.

> retains a kind of imaginal body (*hay'atī az khayāl*), [bearing the forms of whatever the imaginal soul knew or did]. Likewise, reward and punishment are determined for the human soul in proportion to that [imaginal body] and the imaginal soul reminds it of this reward and punishment. The identity (*taʿayyun*) of human souls in the hereafter (*ākhirat*) is determined by this because in this world human beings are spiritual beings clothed in corporeal bodies, while in the next world they are corporeal beings clothed in spirituality.[1]

This characterization of the afterlife departs from Peripatetic eschatology that considers only a spiritual end for the human soul. Ṭūsī's solution for the afterlife through the imaginal power of the soul became a model for eschatology in later Islamic philosophy, most importantly for Mullā Ṣadrā, who copied *Āghāz wa-anjām* in his *Mafātīḥ al-ghayb* without identifying it as an Ismaʿili source.[2] This shows the important influence of Ṭūsī's Ismaʿili writings on later Shiʿa intellectual and spiritual discourses, a fact that is not often admitted by Twelver scholars.

It is clear that Ṭūsī's eschatology is strongly influenced by Suhrawardī, who posits the world of suspended images (*al-ʿālam al-muthul al-muʿallaqa*) as an intermediary world between the corporeal and spiritual worlds. But for Suhrawardī, this is only the final abode of lesser souls where they can 'call forth tastes, forms, pleasant sounds, and the like as they desire'. The higher ranks of souls will enjoy an

1 Ibid., p. 34.

2 See Ḥasan H. Āmulī, *Āghāz wa anjām-i Khawāja Naṣīr al-Dīn Ṭūsī: Muqaddama wa-sharḥ wa-taʿlīqāt*, Tehran: Chāpkhāna-yi Wizārat-i Farhang wa-Irshād-i Islāmī, 1374 S.H./1995.

eternal intellectual bliss.[1] In contrast, Ṭūsī does not delimit the imaginal afterlife to lesser souls alone, and so remains closer to the doctrine of all-embracing resurrection in the Qur'an. Thus, in his *Tajrīd*, Ṭūsī aligns his eschatology with the exoteric teachings of his faith and reinstates the necessity of bodily resurrection according to the Qur'an and Traditions.[2]

Free Will and Determinism

Free will is one of the major topics in Islamic theology and metaphysics, especially in its relation to ethics and to politics in its application and maintenance of justice. It is particularly important in theology with respect to the omniscience and omnipotence of God and to providence (*qaḍā'*), which some theologians interpret as God's foreknowledge of and control over all actions in the world, including human actions. Ashʿarī theologians are recognised for contesting human free will in favour of divine intervention, though there are various interpretations and modifications of this belief among Ashʿarīs. Another group of theologians, broadly categorized as Muʿtazilī, emphasize human free will and argue that it is implicit in divine justice because God would not give humans rewards and punishments for actions over which they have no control. According to the Muʿtazilīs, moral accountability requires free will.

For theologians and philosophers alike, the most challenging question regarding free will has always been whether God knows everything that eventually happens before it actually happens. Muslim thinkers have rarely denied God's omniscience but they have taken different paths to avoid determinism and to reconcile God's fore-

1 Suhrawardī, *The Philosophy of Illumination*, pp. 148–149.
2 Ḥillī, *Kashf al-murād*, p. 380.

knowledge with human free will. For example, Fārābī associates with the indeterminacy of all future events due to the inherent contingency in all actions and events. He argues that this contingency and the resultant indeterminacy are not removed by God's knowledge of the actions and events in eternity.[1] In other words, God's knowledge that something will happen at a point in the future is not the cause of its happening.

For Ibn Sīnā, nothing happens unless it is necessitated by its cause. The physical and metaphysical worlds are equally ruled by necessity. Although human actions based in free will are different from other events in nature because they are intentional, they are still caused and do not issue just randomly. This is not the same as God causing our actions directly or having knowledge of particular events before and during their happening because God only has knowledge of universals. Yet for Ibn Sīnā, the chain of causes in the world finally goes back to God as the true cause of everything that comes to exist, including all events and actions.[2] In this respect, Ibn Sīnā distinguishes between providence and predestination. In his commentary, Ṭūsī defines them as follows:

> Providence (*qaḍā*) is the existence of all things in the intelligible world (*al-ʿālam al-ʿaqlī*) together in a general (*mujmala*) state by way of unmediated creation (*ibdāʿ*).[3] And predestination (*qadar*) is the existence [of

1 See Catarina Belo, 'Freedom and Determinism', in Richard C. Taylor and Luis Xavier López Farjeat, eds., *The Routledge Companion to Islamic Philosophy*, London & New York: Routledge, 2014, p. 331.

2 See Ṭūsī, *Sharḥ al-Ishārāt wa'l-tanbīhāt*, vol. III, p. 297.

3 As the term *ʿibdā'* is not used in an Ismaʿili context here, I have not translated it as 'transcendent innovation', which is my preferred translation for this term in Ismaʿili texts.

> those things] in external matter after the fulfilment of particular conditions one after the other.[1]

All events in the world must therefore be discussed under the second category, that is, '*qadar*'. If, however, according to Ibn Sīnā, God only has knowledge of unchangeable universals, then human choices and actions, being particular events, cannot be considered predetermined in God's knowledge. Yet, all the faculties and powers that the soul is equipped with, including human actions based on free will, are included within the order of God's creations. Here Ṭūsī follows Ibn Sīnā in considering all the causes in the world including the causes of our voluntary actions as intermediary causes that depend on God as the first cause. This is how Ibn Sīnā, and after him Ṭūsī, attempted to reconcile the Aristotelian world of causal necessity with the Islamic doctrine of providence, which is one of the five articles of faith in Sunni Islam. For Ṭūsī this is different from attributing all actions to God as the immediate cause as some Ashᶜarī theologians say.[2]

Shiᶜa theology does not consider the doctrine of providence and predestination (*qaḍā wa-qadar*) to be among the articles of faith. Influenced by Muᶜtazilī rationalism and the Shiᶜa ideology of seeking justice and political reform, Shiᶜa theologians argue that human free will is a state midway between the absolute delegation of power to humans (*tafwīḍ*) and determinism (*jabr*). Ṭūsī cites the sixth Shiᶜa imam, Jaᶜfar al-Ṣādiq, referring to the problem of free will, 'it is neither absolute determinism (*jabr*), nor absolute delegation (*tafwīḍ*) [of power to humankind]; but rather

1 Ṭūsī, *Sharḥ al-Ishārāt wa'l-tanbīhāt*, vol. III, p. 298.
2 Ibid., p. 38.

a state between the two.'[1] As a Shiʿa scholar and ethicist, Ṭūsī opts for this compatibilist approach to free will while also remaining dedicated to Ibn Sīnā's conceptual framework. Ṭūsī's most detailed discussion of the subject is a treatise in Persian titled *Jabr wa-qadar* (Determinism and Predestination). He begins the treatise with a discussion of the rivalry between the believers in absolute determinism (*jabrīs*) and the adherents of absolute freedom (*qadarīs*). He explains that the main argument of the first group is premised on God's foreknowledge, and that that of the second group is based on moral accountability and the rationale for reward and punishment.[2] Next, he gives an account of causality and causal relation by using the Avicennan tripartite analytical tools of necessity (*wujūb*), contingency (*imkān*) and impossibility (*imtināʿ*). For any phenomenon to come into existence, it must be contingent or possible. For example, reading is possible for human beings but not everyone can read. There is a host of other conditions that must be present to necessitate a person's reading. Nothing happens in the world unless it is necessitated (*mūjab*) by sufficient causation. Here, in tandem with Ibn Sīnā's metaphysics, Ṭūsī refutes chance (*ittifāq*) in the sense of a random event and explains that what appears to be random does have a cause of which we are yet unaware.[3] In the same sense, free will is not randomness. In voluntary actions, a person's choice between two courses of action, for example drinking from the blue cup rather than the red cup, is necessitated by

1 Ibid., p. 40. This is my translation of the Arabic citation in the treatise.
2 Ṭūsī, *Jabr wa-qadar*, trans. Parviz Morewedge as 'Determinism and Predestination', in Parviz Morewedge, ed. and trans., *The Metaphysics of Ṭūsī*, New York: The Society for the Study of Islamic Philosophy and Science, 1992, pp. 4–6.
3 Ibid., pp. 7–23.

the determination (*tarjīḥ*) of the agent, which in turn is based on a derterminant or preference (*murajjiḥ*) that causes the choice to be made even though in some cases one may not know what that determinant is. But does this causal necessity contradict free will? Ṭūsī's answer is a categorical 'No':

> The necessity and impossibility cited by us do not negate freewill. This means that the able agent is an agent who is able to perform and able not to perform, meaning that both performance and cessation of activity are appropriate to it and equivalent as options. When a chooser selects an option, the option is realized. Thus, if preference (*murajjiḥ*) is his choice, whenever he chooses, he acts; whenever he does not choose [to act], he does not. This is called a voluntary agent (*mukhtār*). It is evident from this argument that a free [agent] has two features: one, power (*qudrat*); the other, will (*irādat*). Power means acting and ceasing to act [are both options of the agent]; he never has only one of these options. Will is that which when joined with power implies preference of an action, which means that when power and will exist, the realization of an action is necessary and the lack of action is an impossibility.[1]

After explaining the role of preference in voluntary actions and the difference between voluntary and involuntary actions, Ṭūsī enquires into the origin of the will. He argues that upon encountering different options, the soul—with the aid of imagination and the intellect, which present it with the possible benefits of each choice—desires

1 Ibid., p. 25.

one of them. The desire (*shawq*) mobilizes the faculties of the soul and the body towards a particular course of action.[1] Thus, from an ethical point of view, moral responsibilities, judgements, rewards and punishments are meaningful only in light of the desire for some perfection and the ensuing will (*irādat*) and attempt (*jahd*) towards achieving it.

To sum up, all the faculties and powers that the soul is equipped with are included within the order of God's creations. Ṭūsī follows Ibn Sīnā in considering all the causes in the world, including the causes of our voluntary actions, as intermediary causes that depend on God as the first cause. Yet he also contends this is different from attributing all actions to God as the immediate cause as some Ashᶜarī theologians say.[2] Human beings are destined by God to make voluntary choices and to make an attempt towards them, and that is the reason why certain actions cannot be issued without an attempt. This line of argument is used by most Shiᶜa scholars who believe that there is a middle path between absolute determinism and absolute freedom. Ṭūsī cites the sixth Shiᶜa imam, Jaᶜfar al-Ṣādiq, referring to the problem of free will that 'it is neither absolute determinism (*jabr*), nor absolute delegation (*tafwīḍ*) [of power to humankind]; but rather a state between the two.'[3] Thus, Ṭūsī uses Ibn Sīnā's philosophy of free will to prove the Shiᶜa position on this controversial issue, and this line of argument becomes a model for later Shiᶜa theologians and philosophers.

A Logical Philosopher

Ṭūsī's logical writings are too concentrated and specialized

1 Ibid., pp. 31–34.
2 Ibid., p. 38.
3 Ibid., p. 40. This statement is my translation of the Arabic citation in the treatise.

for an introductory volume, but a discussion of his theoretical wisdom would be incomplete without introducing some of the hallmarks of his contributions to logic. While modelling his study of logic on Ibn Sīnā, Ṭūsī also relies on other thinkers, most importantly, Abu'l-Barakāt al-Baghdādī (d. ca. 560/1165). Ṭūsī's major work on logic is written in Persian and its title, *Asās al-iqtibās* (Foundation of the Derivation), suggests that for Ṭūsī logic is the foundation of all other forms of wisdom (*ḥikmat*).[1] This work is one of the most extensive and rigorous logical treatises in the Muslim world alongside Ibn Sīnā's *Manṭiq al-Shifā* (The Logic of the Healing) and the commentaries on Aristotle's logic by the Andalusian Muslim philosopher Ibn Rushd. Following Ibn Sīnā, Ṭūsī concentrates on the Aristotelian-Peripatetic divisions in the study of logic. He defines the science of logic as 'knowledge of those notions (*maʿānī*) through which one may possibly reach all kinds of acquired sciences (*ʿulūm-i muktasab*) and know what particular science each notion leads to.'[2] In the introduction to *Asās al-iqtibās*, Ṭūsī's study of these notions is derived from Porphyry's (d. ca. 305 CE) *Isagoge*, which Islamic philosophers considered as *the* introduction to the study of logic and philosophy. Based on the connection between language and logic, the *Isagoge* divides all predicables (*maqūlāt*) into five universal terms (*al-kulliyyāt al-khams*): genus (*jins*), difference (*faṣl*), species (*nawʿ*), special property (*khāṣṣa*) and common property (*ʿaraḍ-i ʿāmm*). The five predicables are the principles for defining and knowing things in the world, hence their importance as a link between language and metaphysics. They signify the essential and accidental properties of things. For example, in the

1 Sayyid ʿAbd Allāh Anwār, *Taʿlīqa bar Asās al-iqtibās-i Khwāja Naṣīr-i Ṭūsī*, Tehran: Nashr-i Markaz, 1996, vol. 1, p. 18.
2 Ibid., p. 19.

Peripatetic tradition, a human being is defined as a rational animal, with 'animal' as the 'genus' and 'rational' as the difference. These two terms indicate the essential properties of the human 'species' without which no individual instance of the species can be called human. Conversely, accidental properties may or may not actually exist for an instance of a species. For example, according to Ṭūsī, laughing is a special property of the human species because it is exclusive to it, while moving around on feet is a common property that humans share with some animals. Neither property is essential to the human species because a human being can be human and recognised as human without them.[1]

Having defined the five universal terms and the divisions within each on the basis of Porphyry's *Isagoge*, Ṭūsī prepares the reader for the next chapters whose subjects follow Aristotle's *Organon*. The chapters are: 1) *Categories* explains the ten Aristotelian categories of reality that are discussed in logic as universals or intelligibles in distinction to each other as substance and nine accidents. Here, Ṭūsī demonstrates an awareness of the metaphysical status of the categories but argues that they should still be discussed under logic because 'it would be impossible to acquire the premises (*muqaddamāt*) of syllogisms (*qīyāsāt*) without conceiving the categories that are the ultimate genuses (*ajnās-i ʿāliya*) in their distinction from each other.'[2] 2) *De Interpretatione*, begins with semantics which explores the relation between language, mind and the world. Ṭūsī demarcates layers of signification (*dalālāt*): the signification of external entities by mental forms or concepts, the signification of mental forms or concepts by oral linguistic utterances and the sig-

1 Ibid., pp. 37–39.
2 Ibid., p. 42.

nification of linguistic utterances by written words.[1] This is followed by several sections on different kinds of statements (*qaḍāyā*) and their logical relations with each other, truth conditions and modalities. 3) *Prior Analytics* examines different types of syllogism (*qīyās*) that Ṭūsī defines as a necessary implication of an affirmative statement or conclusion from two other affirmative statements or premises.[2] 4) *Posterior Analytics* is divided into two parts: apodictic demonstration (*burhān*) and definition (*ḥadd*). The first part of the chapter includes epistemological discussions such as the objects, scope and principles of knowledge, as well as epistemic justification and conditions of certitude (*yaqīn*). Ṭūsī also discusses in detail the role of sense perception and induction in empirical knowledge. In the sections on definition, he explains different kinds of definition in light of their essential and accidental components. He also discusses the relation between linguistic components in a definition and their relation to the external world by tracing the formal and material causes of the subject of the definition. 5) *Topics* discusses the nature and value of dialectical argument (*jadal*). 6) *Sophistics* offers a detailed discussion of different kinds of fallacies (*mughāliṭāt*).

In addition to these parts that correspond to the *Organon*, Ṭūsī also follows the Arabic tradition of including *Rhetoric* and *Poetics* in his logical compendium. They make up the last two chapters of the book. Thus, the content of the *Asās al-iqtibās* justifies Ṭūsī's choice of the title, *Foundation of the Derivation*, since it covers the principles of metaphysics, epistemology, empirical sciences, semantics, rhetoric and poetry based on a study of language and logic.

One of the areas in Peripatetic logic that overlaps with

1 Ibid., pp. 60–61.
2 Ibid., p. 140.

physics and metaphysics is the *Categories*, especially the discussion of substance (*jawhar*). Traditionally, 'substance' is defined as a 'thing', which is not in a 'subject' (*mawḍūʿ*). Substance is that which, if it exists, does not need a subject for its actual subsistence in reality.[1] In the *Categories* section of *Asās al-iqtibās*, Ṭūsī is credited with using an analytical approach that distinguishes between science and metaphysics in relation to 'substance'. While emphasizing the distinction between 'primary substances' (*jawāhir-i awwalī*) that exist individually and 'secondary substances' (*jawāhir-i thānīya*) that are universals such as genus and species,[2] Ṭūsī, in his differentiation between the natural sciences and philosophy, 'is less involved in an "ontological inquiry" than in a syntactical conceptual inquiry'.[3] So while reviewing the principles of speculative and natural sciences, Ṭūsī also offers methodological clarifications for studying the same subjects in different areas.

In addition to *Asās al-iqtibās*, Ṭūsī has a shorter treatise on logic in Arabic, *Tajrīd al-manṭiq* (The Summa of Logic). The treatise concisely covers all the sections of logic listed above including rhetoric and poetry. The famous scholar and disciple of Ṭūsī ʿAllāma Ḥillī (d. 726/1325) has a commentary on this treatise titled *al-Jawhar al-naḍīd* (The Substantial Core [of *Asās al-Iqtibās*]). To this treatise, an appendix was later added by the Safavid philosopher Mullā Ṣadrā Shīrāzī entitled *Taṣawwur wa-taṣdīq* (Conception and Affirmation). The numerous other scholarly studies in Ṭūsī's works on logic prove the significance of his contri-

1 Ibid., p. 43.
2 Ibid., p. 44.
3 Parviz Morewedge, 'The Analysis of Substance in Ṭūsī's Logic', in George F. Hourani, ed. *Essays on Islamic Philosophy and Science*, Albany: State University of New York Press, 1975, p. 176.

bution to the subject. In addition to the depth and clarity of his logical discussions, his works are also important for concurrently discussing the views of the classical and later logicians. This quality is mentioned by Ḥillī in his introduction to his *al-Jawhar al-naḍīd*. Ḥillī states that the treatise 'covers in a refined language noble subjects whose meaning and content are hard to fathom, and brings together the words of earlier scholars and what was added by their successors...'[1]

To summarize, Ṭūsī's logical writings are more than just expository works. Building on the work of his predecessors in the field, he contributes to the study of logic by making critical points, expanding on certain topics, and creating methodological subtleties that help demarcate disciplines through logical analysis.

Master of Exact Sciences

Ṭūsī worked in several scientific areas but he is famous mainly for his geometrical and astronomical studies. Since the discovery of Ṭūsī's texts by the West in the nineteenth century and the translation of some parts of his *Tadhkira fī ʿilm al-hay'a* (Memoir on the Science of Astronomy), scholars have tried to place his work within the context of the scientific changes that led to the Copernican Revolution. To assess the scope of Ṭūsī's influence on the Latin West is beyond the confines of the present work, and so is a proper analysis of his ventures into mathematics, geometry and astronomy. What follows is only a brief overview of his scientific achievements.

The composition date of the *Tadhkira fī ʿilm al-hay'a*

1 Muḥammad al-Muṭahhar al-Ḥillī, *al-Jawhar al-naḍīd fī sharḥ manṭiq al-tajrīd*, ed. Muḥsin Bīdārfar, Tehran: Intishārāt-i Bīdār, 1363 s.h./1984, p. 6.

(659/1261) gives the false impression that Ṭūsī's interest in astronomy and his attempts to modify Ptolemy's planetary model began during the later period of his life when he was in charge of the Marāgha Observatory. In fact, Ṭūsī had already authored two works on astronomy early in his life: *Risāla-yi Muʿīniyya dar hay'a* (The *Muʿīniyya* Treatise on Astronomy) and *Ḥall-i mushkilāt-i Muʿīniyya* (Solutions for the Problems of the *Muʿīniyya*). These texts demonstrate the depth of his knowledge in both Euclidean geometry and Aristotelian physics. Thanks also to recent scholarship, we now know that Ṭūsī was concerned with finding solutions to some of the problems in Ptolemy's model much earlier when he was living among the Ismaʿilis. According to Jamil Ragep, long before working at the Marāgha Observatory, Ṭūsī had solved some of the problems of Ptolemy's model that had been identified by the famous medieval Muslim scientist Ibn al-Haytham (d. ca. 430/1040).[1] Ṭūsī's interest in Ptolemy's model was a result of his actual astronomical observations and the discrepancies he found between them and the Ptolemaic model.

In fact, Ṭūsī's contributions to astronomy are celebrated primarily for his attempts to modify Ptolemy's planetary model by introducing what is known as 'the Ṭūsī Couple', a set of mathematical devices. Broadly speaking, the set consists of two circles, one twice the other in diameter, where the smaller one rotates inside the larger one. The two circles move in opposite directions with a uniform motion while the smaller circle rotates twice as fast as the larger circle. The mathematical configuration made by the position and

1 F. Jamil Ragep, 'The Two Versions of the Ṭūsī Couple', in *From Deferent to Equant: A Volume of Studies in the History of Science in the Ancient and Medieval Near East in Honour of E. S. Kennedy*, New York: New York Academy of Sciences, 1987, p. 331.

motion of the two circles explains the oscillation of the epicycle centre in the Ptolemaic lunar model. The Epicycle was Ptolemy's model for explaining the changes in the speed and direction of planets, but it contained several limitations. The Ṭūsī Couple was an attempt to remove some of these limitations from the Epicycle model and it was most successful in this with regard to the moon. For example, it helped explain 'the variation in the lunar distance from the centre of the earth, without disturbing longitudinal variations.'[1] It is not possible to cover the technicalities of the model here since it requires mathematical and scientific expertise. For the purpose of the present discussion, it is sufficient to add that the Ṭūsī Couple was subject to further interpretations and developments both in the East and in the West. It also earned Ṭūsī the privilege of having a crater of the Moon named after him, 'Nasireddin'.

In the West, the appearance of the Ṭūsī Couple and its impact on the development of astronomy were not due to the translation of Ṭūsī's works into Latin but rather to what Jamil Ragep calls 'intercultural transmissions' or to 'nonextant texts or nontextual transmissions.'[2] As for Ṭūsī's scientific influence within Islamicate cultures, it has been conclusively demonstrated that most astronomical studies during the Ottoman Empire (699–1342/1299–1923) were based on Ṭūsī's *Tadhkira* and its commentaries. In addition to the *Tadhkira*, other texts by Ṭūsī were translated into Turkish by Ottoman

1 George Saliba & E. S. Kenney, 'The Spherical Case of the Ṭūsī Couple', in N. Pourjavady and Ž. Vesel, eds., *Naṣīr al-Dīn Ṭūsī: Philosophe et Savant du XIIIe Siècle*, Tehran: Institut Français de Recherche en Iran, 2000, p. 106.
2 F. Jamil Ragep, 'From Tūn to Turuń: The Twists and Turns of the Ṭūsī-Couple', in Rivka Feldhay and F. Jamil Ragep, eds., *Before Copernicus: The Cultural Contexts of Scientific Learning in the Fifteenth Century*, Montreal & Kingston, Canada: McGill-Queen's University Press, 2017, pp. 174–175.

scholars and were widely used as textbooks. Among these was *Sī faṣl dar maʿrifat-i taqwīm* (Thirty Chapters on Knowledge of the Calendar); it was translated in around 1421 and was used as a textbook in astronomy and the creation of calendars.[1] Another influential text by Ṭūsī was his annotated edition of Euclid's *Elements of Geometry* entitled *Taḥrīr kitāb uṣūl al-hindisa li Uqlīdus* (A Recension of the *Book of Elements of Geometry* by Euclid). This work was a valuable source for the study and teaching of Euclidean geometry during the Ottoman times.[2]

Aside from his works on astronomy and geometry, Ṭūsī also produced a treatise in Persian titled *Tansūkh-nāma-yi īlkhānī* (The Khan's Book of Precious Goods), which focuses primarily on mineralogy but also includes several sections on other substances of value such as ivory and medicinal plants. The main sources for this treatise are *al-Jamāhir fī maʿrifat al-jawāhir* (Essentials of the Knowledge of Precious Substances) by the famous Muslim scientist Abū Rayḥān Bīrūnī (d. ca. 442/1050), and *Jawāhir-nāma-yi Niẓāmī* (Niẓāmī's Book on Precious Gems) by Muḥammad Jawharī Naysābūrī (d. 592/1195–6).[3] *Tansūkh-nāma* opens with the author's praise for the Creator of all the precious things in the world and an acknowledgment that the book was written at the request of a Mongol king who is not mentioned by name. The first discourse (*maqālat*) begins

1 Salim Aydüz, 'Naṣīr al-Dīn Ṭūsī's Influence on Ottoman Scientific Literature (Mathematics, Astronomy, Natural Sciences)', *Intl. J. Turkish Studies*, vol. XVII, nos. 1 & 2, 2011, pp. 23–24.

2 Ibid., pp. 25–27.

3 See Ž. Vesel, I. Afshar, et al., '*Le livre des pierres pour Neẓāmī* [Al-Molk]: La source présumée du *Tansūkh-Nāmaye Īlkhānī* de Ṭūsī', in N. Pourjavady and Ž. Vesel, eds., *Naṣīr al-Dīn Ṭūsī Philosophe et Savant du XIIIe Siècle*, Tehran: Institut Français de Recherche en Iran, 2000, pp. 145–150.

with the cause of the existence of the four elements, followed by a chapter about the origins of gems (*jawāhir*), and two other chapters on their solidity (*taḥajjur*) and colour. The second and longest part of the book discusses different kinds of gems; the third part is dedicated to seven metallic elements and the last part examines aromatic substances and medicinal plants such as saffron. *Tansūkh-nāma* has a very clear structure and language usage; these, together with its scientific content, must have contributed significantly to its wide-reaching transmission across both Persian and Turkish regions.

With this brief review of the scientific aspects of Ṭūsī's career, we reach the end of the chapter on his work on theoretical wisdom. As previously mentioned, all the areas of Ṭūsī's work form a whole so there continue to be strong philosophical and scientific elements present in his writings related to what is called practical wisdom in the next chapter.

CHAPTER TWO
Practical Wisdom

Ṭūsī's views on knowledge and free will have been discussed above under theoretical wisdom. Connected to knowledge and free will is moral responsibility, which falls under practical wisdom. In Islamic philosophy the human soul is destined for greatness and can transcend its animal aspects by fulfilling the potential within rationality. The application or fulfilment of rationality happens at both the theoretical and practical levels. Theory and practice are intertwined and come into fruition only if they reinforce each other. These are the major premises on which Ṭūsī builds his practical philosophy, and they are informed by several intellectual discourses, namely, Peripatetic philosophy, Muʿtazilī theology and Ismaʿilism. This comes as no surprise because Ṭūsī writes as a philosopher, a Shiʿa Muslim and a scholar of Ismaʿili thought. As a philosopher, Ṭūsī writes within the Peripatetic framework of the Neoplatonic readings of Aristotle as established by Fārābī and Ibn Sīnā. As a Shiʿa Muslim, he prefers Muʿtazilī theology that centres on free will and justice. As an Ismaʿili scholar, he considers any kind of wisdom, including practical wisdom, to be dependent on the instruction of the imam or his representative.

The classic division of practical wisdom into ethics,

economics and politics determines the structure of *Akhlāq-i Nāṣirī* (The Nasirean Ethics), Ṭūsī's major work on practical wisdom. The *Akhlāq* is one of his main compositions during his time among the Ismaʿilis. He started the project at the request of the Chief (*Muḥtasham*) of Quhistān, Nāṣir al-Dīn, and named it after him. He also dedicated another treatise on ethics to the Muḥtasham, *Akhlāq-i Muḥtashamī*. The two treatises are, however, different in structure, scope, content and sources.

There are two editions of *Akhlāq-i Nāṣirī* each with different preambles; the second edition contains a disavowal of Ṭūsī's praise for the Ismaʿilis found in the first preamble. Ṭūsī revised the first preamble after his departure from the Ismaʿili fortresses as part of his attempt to exonerate himself from affinity with the Ismaʿilis. Considering that the book was commissioned by the Ismaʿili Chief, the replacement of the preamble sounds rather unethical, which is ironic for a book on ethics. Yet, as previously mentioned, Ṭūsī's biography shows that survival was always a priority for him. Moreover, in Shiʿism the rule of dissimulation or concealment of true beliefs (*taqiyya*) as a method of self-protection was devised to preserve one's life under hostile circumstances. There is no conclusive evidence that Ṭūsī ever converted to Ismaʿilism and if he did, whether or not he remained an adherent after leaving the Ismaʿili fortresses. What cannot be contested is that Ṭūsī's writings contributed greatly to the development and growth of Ismaʿili ideas and discourse.

Ṭūsī's *Akhlāq-i Nāṣirī* is one of his most influential works. The wide scope of subjects and sources in this long treatise has made it a model for writings on practical wisdom in mediaeval philosophical literature in the Muslim world; though it could be seen as rivalling the more 'orthodox' treatises on Islamic ethics which are dependent exclusively on Islamic law (*Sharīʿa*), the Qur'an and the Traditions. The treatise is also important for its linguistic medium, Persian. During his sojourn among the Ismaʿilis, Ṭūsī wrote several treatises in Persian that reveal the importance of Persian identity to the Ismaʿili governors who were contesting the Arab hegemony of the time. The *Akhlāq-i Nāṣirī* was originally commissioned to be a translation into Persian of *Kitāb al-tahāra* (the Book of Purification)—mostly known as *Tahdhīb al-akhlāq* (The Refinement of Character)—by the Twelver scholar Ibn Miskawayh (d. 421/1030). Yet, only the first part of *Akhlāq-i Nāṣirī*, namely the part on ethics, is based on Ibn Miskawayh's *Tahdhīb al-akhlāq*. The other two topics of practical philosophy—economics and politics—which make up parts two and three of *Akhlāq-i Nāṣirī*, were not addressed by Ibn Miskawayh. In the rest of his treatise, Ṭūsī freely cites Greek philosophers, sometimes erroneously, as well as citing Fārābī and Ibn Sīnā. One can also see the mathematical and scientific edge of Ṭūsī's thought in this book in his frequent use of such concepts as symmetry, relations among numbers, equilibrium and balance in nature. According to Wilferd Madelung, all the three parts of the book are replete with philosophical citations that show that the Ismaʿilis did not regard philosophy and religion as being incompatible.[1]

In Ṭūsī's other treatise on ethics, *Akhlāq-i Muḥtashamī*, the reliance on philosophical citations found in *Akhlāq-i Nāṣirī* is replaced by religious citations. Though written in the same context as *Akhlāq-i Nāṣirī* and based on a manuscript originally drafted by his patron, the Chief of Quhistān, this book does not have a philosophical character and for the most part its content is religious. It is abundant

1 Wilferd Madelung, 'Naṣīr al-Dīn Ṭūsī's Ethics between Philosophy, Shiʿism, and Sufism', p. 71.

with citations from the Qur'an and Prophetic and Shiʿa traditions. The ethics presented in this book is primarily religious ethics or a set of rules for righteousness presented in an aphoristic style based on sacred and didactic literature. Compared to the sophisticated content and style of *Akhlāq-i Nāṣirī*, this work clearly addresses a different audience with its simple style and topics that resonate with familiar Islamic and Shiʿa beliefs. In short, *Akhlāq-i Muḥtashamī* is mostly concerned with moral behaviour as it determines the quality of faith and drawing near to God. As for its religious sources, in addition to the Qur'an and Traditions, it cites from major Shiʿa texts such as *Nahj al-balāgha* by ʿAlī b. Abī Ṭālib, the first Shiʿa imam, and *al-Ṣaḥīfa al-sajjādiyya* by ʿAlī b. al-Ḥusayn Zayn al-ʿĀbidīn, the fourth Shiʿa imam. Its main source for Shiʿa traditions is *Uṣūl al-kāfī*, which is the earliest collection of Shiʿa traditions compiled by Muḥammad Yaʿqūb al-Kulaynī (d. 329/864). Ṭūsī's citation of non-Islamic texts in *Akhlāq-i Muḥtashamī* is confined to some quick words of wisdom by Greek philosophers and quotations from other widely read didactic texts; these appear only at the end of each chapter. Nowhere in the book does the author offer a philosophical argument. This holds true even in the case of shared topics between the two books, such as happiness and friendship.

Apart from these two major works on ethics, Ṭūsī also translated Ibn al-Muqaffā's *al-Adab al-wajīz li'l-walad al-ṣaghīr* (A Short Manual on Ethical Behaviour for the Young Child).[1] This book is proof of Ṭūsī's interest in all areas of ethics, as well as his acknowledgment of the connection between ethics and education. It has a rather

1 For a summary of this book, see Dabashi, 'Khwājah Naṣīr al-Dīn Ṭūsī: the Philosopher/Vizier and the Intellectual Climate of his Times', pp. 561–562.

conformist and conservative agenda advising children to abide by the understanding of those in authority of the time and by the opinions of the majority.

Ethics

As mentioned above, the main source for understanding Ṭūsī's ethics is his *Akhlāq-i Nāṣirī* due to its systematic character, width of scope and philosophical content. In the preamble of the book, Ṭūsī already sets out its philosophical character by stating that the topics covered in *Akhlāq-i Nāṣirī* fall under the practical division of philosophy. He further explains that the division of philosophy into theory and practice is because the function of philosophy itself is 'to know things as they are and to fulfil functions as one should'.[1] Both divisions of philosophy serve human beings in their path towards perfection by actualizing the potential of the soul. In tandem with his Greek and Muslim philosophical predecessors, Ṭūsī puts 'perfection' (*kamāl*) at the centre of his discourse on knowledge and action. His subdivisions of theoretical and practical philosophy follow Fārābī's classification of sciences in his *Iḥṣā' al-ʿulūm* (Enumeration of Sciences), which covered all sciences of the time. Ṭūsī holds that practical philosophy facilitates the achievement of perfection in human life both individually and communally in this world and the next.[2] This explains the wide scope of the book, which includes topics ranging from individual manners to civic disciplines and judicial norms.

Thus, in *Akhlāq-i Nāṣirī*, ethics consists of the manners and disciplines that guide the individual soul towards

1 Ṭūsī, *Akhlāq-i Nāṣirī*, trans. G. M. Wickens as *The Nasirean Ethics*, London & New York: Routledge, 1964, p. 27.
2 Ibid., p. 28.

its perfection. The first chapter on ethics follows Ibn Miskawayh's *Tahdhīb al-akhlāq* and opens with the definition of the human soul and its faculties. Ṭūsī then diverges from Ibn Miskawayh, who discusses love and friendship under ethics. He places these two topics under politics, which is the third part of *Akhlāq-i Nāṣirī*.

As Majid Fakhry correctly noted, Ṭūsī's characterization of the soul is grounded more in Ibn Sīnā's Aristotelian psychology than in Ibn Miskawayh's.[1] Ṭūsī defines the soul as a simple substance that is not the body but governs the body by means of its diverse faculties. Following Ibn Sīnā, he argues that our knowledge of the soul is immediate and intuitive; therefore, we do not need proof for its existence. For example, Ṭūsī states that 'the self is always with the self. Therefore, the utterance of a proof for one's own self is absurd.'[2] He also seems to take for granted the existence of other souls simply based on his own intuitive perception of a rational substance that is not identical with the body while controlling it and functioning as the receptor of intelligibles and the agent of voluntary choices.

Taking as self-evident the existence of the soul, Ṭūsī proceeds to prove its substantiality, simplicity or indivisibility, incorporeality, self-awareness and its survival after the death of the body. In Islamic philosophy, ethical codes are often deduced from premises based on these principles. In the context of ethics, these features form premises based on which ethical principles prove to be necessary. For Ṭūsī, any rule of ethics makes sense when we are dealing, firstly, with a rational agent with the capacity of acquiring knowledge and which in its very essence is independent of the body and can control it; secondly, with an agent that both

1 Majid Fakhry, *Ethical Theories in Islam*, Leiden: Brill, 1994, p. 132.
2 Ṭūsī, *The Nasirean Ethics*, p. 36.

'knows itself and knows that it knows itself;'[1] thirdly, with an agent that will not perish along with the body. As for the details of the soul-body relationship, Ṭūsī refers us to natural philosophy.

As an example of Ṭūsī's style of argumentation in this treatise, this is a summary of his argument for the incorporeality of the soul: 1) Each bodily organ can only receive its own sensibles and has no judgement over the soundness of its perception. 2) The rational soul perceives sensibles from all bodily organs and can distinguish between sound perceptions and erroneous ones as in the case of sensory errors and illusions. 3) The rational soul cannot have received these powers from the bodily organs because they cannot give what they do not have in the first place. Therefore, the rational soul is other than the corporeal body.[2]

Ṭūsī closes the section on the nature of the rational soul by reminding the reader that his goal in expounding on such matters is to dismiss the naturalistic approach to the soul where the body is the necessary locus (*maḥall*) of the soul. He emphasizes that the rational soul is independent of the body and only uses the body as a tool. With this view of the soul in mind, Ṭūsī briefly presents the faculties of the soul through synthetic argument based on Plato, Aristotle and the Qur'an. While Ibn Miskawayh maintains Plato's tripartite division of the soul into the rational, the concupiscent and the irascible,[3] Ṭūsī addresses the division within the Aristotelian framework while finding a place also for the Platonic faculties. For Ṭūsī, as for Ibn Sīnā, there are

1 Ibid., p. 39.
2 Ibid.
3 Ibn Miskawayh, *Tahdhīb al-akhlāq*, trans. Constantine K. Zurayk as *The Refinement of Character*, Beirut: Great Books of the Islamic World Inc., 2002, pp. 14–15.

three types of souls, namely, the vegetative soul, the animal soul and the human soul. To these, Ṭūsī adds the Platonic faculties by making the rational soul a subdivision of the human soul, and the concupiscent and the irascible souls as subdivisions of the faculty of voluntary motion, which is in turn a subdivision of the animal soul.[1] The Platonic faculties also reappear later under a section on the perfection of the human soul. There, Ṭūsī identifies the rational, the irascible, and the concupiscent souls with the Qur'anic division of the human soul into the peaceful soul (*al-nafs al-muṭma'inna*), the reproachful soul (*al-nafs al-lawwāma*) and the imperative soul (*al-nafs al-ammāra*). In this discussion of Qur'anic terms, Ṭūsī makes several direct and indirect allusions to Plato.[2] By incorporating the Qur'anic narrative of the soul into his overall discussion of the soul, Ṭūsī prepares the groundwork for bridging Greek metaphysical psychology with a psychology that is more acceptable to a religious mind frame.

The short section on the soul's faculties is followed by a longer section on the superiority of the human soul over all the other beings in the world. Ṭūsī formulates a hierarchy based on different combinations and configurations of elements beginning with the inanimate world at the bottom to organic life, with plants, animals and finally human beings as the pinnacle of existence. Ṭūsī's narrative here is reminiscent of the doctrine of degrees of excellence (*tafāḍul*) that frequently appears in Fatimid Ismaʿili literature. He stratifies every species into different ranks, the highest of which verges on the next higher species. For example, the palm tree is the noblest among plants and a transition to the animal species, and the horse, due to its high potential

1 Ṭūsī, *The Nasirean Ethics*, pp. 41–43.
2 Ibid., pp. 57–58.

to receive instruction, is the highest rank of animal and connects the animal species to the human species. This argument and the examples given, namely the palm tree and the horse, are most likely adaptations from *Ithbāt al-imāma* (Proof of the Imamate) by the Fatimid thinker Aḥmad b. Ibrāhīm Naysābūrī (fl. 5th/11th).[1] Thus Ṭūsī's emphasis on instruction in the example of the horse makes this section of the text congruent with his Ismaʿili narratives because 'instruction' (*taʿlīm*) is an important component of Ismaʿili ideology.

As for the human species, after arguing that ranks of perfection among human beings are determined according to will and reason and that 'the ennobling of their virtue is entrusted to their reflection, reason, intelligence and will,' Ṭūsī mentions the necessity for 'prophets, philosophers, imams, guides, tutors and instructors'.[2] This is the most obvious example of the way Ṭūsī moves between philosophical and Ismaʿili narratives in his ethics. In contrast to Ṭūsī, Ibn Miskawayh touches on the degrees of excellence among species quite briefly and although he uses the example of the horse and emphasizes its capacity to receive training,[3] the text lacks any Ismaʿili undertones and Ibn Miskawayh does not deduce from the analogy the necessity for an instructor in the sense of a prophet, philosopher or imam.

Apart from his use of Ismaʿili narratives, Ṭūsī also makes

1 See Aḥmad b. Ibrāhīm Naysābūrī, *Ithbāt al-imāma*, ed. and trans. Arzina R. Lalani as *Degrees of Excellence: A Fatimid Treatise on Leadership in Islam*, London: I. B. Tauris, 2010, pp. 46–47. Also see Ḥamīd al-Dīn Kirmānī, *Maṣābīḥ fī ithbāt al-imāma*, ed. and trans. Paul. E. Walker as *Master of the Age: An Islamic Treatise on the Necessity of the Imamate*, New York: I. B. Tauris, 2007, pp. 69–70.

2 Ṭūsī, *The Nasirean Ethics*, pp. 47–48.

3 Ibn Miskawayh, *The Refinement of Character*, p. 42.

use of Sufi narratives. In the following passage from a section on the perfection of the human soul, Ṭūsī attributes the status of sainthood (*wilāya*) and vice-regency of God (*khilāfat Allāh*) to a perfect human (*al-insān al-kāmil*) who has reached the zenith of theoretical and practical wisdom:

> ...When practice becomes his familiar, so that his operations and acts are realized in accordance with acceptable faculties and habits, he becomes a world unto himself, comparable to this macrocosm (*ʿālam-i kabīr*) and merits to be called a microcosm (*ʿālam-i ṣaghīr*). Thus he becomes Almighty God's vice-regent (*khalīfa-yi khudā-yi taʿālā*) among his creatures, entering among his particular Saints (*awliyā-yi khāṣṣ*) and standing as Complete and Absolute Man (*insān-i tāmm-i muṭlaq*).[1]

For Ṭūsī, all his discourses on human perfection converge on the two key topics in his ethics, that is, happiness or felicity (*saʿāda*) and virtue (*faḍīla*).

Happiness and Virtue

For Ṭūsī, happiness (*saʿāda*) is the purpose of the soul's perfection. He also believes that happiness in the true sense of the term can be attributed only to human life because the presence of reason is a necessary condition for the achievement of happiness.[2] This section on happiness in the *Akhlāq-i Nāṣirī* is rich in references to different Greek and Muslim philosophers.

Ṭūsī uses the terms 'happiness' and 'good' interchangeably. His understanding of the good is based on a division of

1 Ṭūsī, *The Nasirean Ethics*, p. 52.
2 Ibid., pp. 59–60.

the good into absolute (*khayr-i muṭlaq*) and relative (*khayr bi iḍāfat*) good, a legacy of Plato's metaphysics and Aristotle's ethics. Absolute good is good in itself and not a medium for attaining another good. All other 'goods' are approximations of the absolute good. Relative good is always a partial good on the way towards the absolute good. All intellectual and moral aspirations of human beings are potentially directed towards the absolute good;[1] the partial goods are the virtues that are necessary for the attainment of final happiness. Here, Ṭūsī follows Aristotle in connecting happiness with virtue. But Ṭūsī uses a variety of other references too including Qur'anic ones—where the absolute good must also follow the will of God[2]—and Neoplatonic ideas—where the body is irrelevant to ultimate and perfect happiness though improving the state of the body is an important partial good.

As for the virtues, Ṭūsī follows Ibn Miskawayh in ranking them starting with the good of the body and moving up to the good of the body and soul together, and lastly, an approximation to the divine good. At the first level of virtue, a person preserves the equilibrium between passions and appetites. In this state, the person does not attain higher spiritual values but simply strives not to fall out of humanity into animality through a life of excessive sensuality. This rank of virtue is a regulatory one and the person learns to remain within the limits of a reasonable lifestyle by avoiding excesses.[3] While being modelled on Aristotle's thesis of virtue as a golden mean, the text also has undertones of the Qur'anic moral dualism according to which the human being is capable of becoming either a beast or rising above the angels.

1 Ibid., pp. 60–61.
2 Ibid.
3 Ibid., p. 66.

At the second level of virtue, one employs 'will and aspiration in the more excellent matter of improving the state of the soul and body, not being involved with passions and appetites.' At this level, the person is in full control of reason and seeks divine things without any expectation of recompense. This level of moral and spiritual achievement can lead to the highest level of virtue at which one imitates the acts of God and this is the ultimate good beyond which one seeks no other good.[1]

Following Plato and Ibn Miskawayh, Ṭūsī classifies the virtues based on the division of the soul into rational, irascible and appetitive. The three corresponding virtues of wisdom, courage and continence are in order when the motion of each aspect of the soul is in 'equilibrium'. Wisdom is the result of equilibrium in the rational soul; courage is the result of equilibrium in the irascible soul; and continence is present when equilibrium is achieved in the appetitive soul. A lack of equilibrium in the motions of the soul will result in the vices that are the opposites of the above virtues. Finally, 'a harmonious blending' of the three virtues results in a fourth class of virtue, justice (*ᶜadl*), which 'represents the perfection and completion' of them all.[2]

After outlining the main virtues, Ṭūsī proceeds to give detailed subdivisions for them with examples; he also enumerates the opposite vices. Many of the virtues and vices are the same as those found in Aristotle's *Nicomachean Ethics*. In imitation of Ibn Miskawayh, Ṭūsī also introduces a category of false virtues, or what he characterizes as 'those states that resemble virtues'; he attributes these to people whose practice resembles wisdom, courage, continence and justice though

1 Ṭūsī, *The Nasirean Ethics*, pp. 66–67.
2 Ibid., pp. 79–80.

they do not practise these virtues for their own sake but for other purposes. For example, some people may act in a manner that resembles continence, but in fact they avoid certain pleasures with the hope of receiving something greater in quality or quantity in this life or in the Hereafter. Or, they may simply be lacking in the capacity to enjoy certain sensations due to internal or external conditions.

Finally, Ṭūsī mentions another condition for genuine virtue and this is when it proceeds from a wise person. An act is genuinely courageous if it issues from a wise person because it is wisdom that employs every virtue 'in its [right] place, in its [right] time, and in a measure required in accordance with best interest.'[1] In this context, Ṭūsī mentions ᶜAlī b. Abī Ṭālib, the first Shiᶜa imam, as an example of a person possessing genuine virtues due to the fulfilment of all the requirements of virtue in him.

The Superiority of Justice

Ṭūsī's focus on the superiority of the virtue of justice can be said to result from the influence of Plato on him and from the Muᶜtazilī emphasis on justice. But justice is also a pivotal doctrine of faith in Shiᶜism. In Shiᶜa theology, justice has technically replaced the Sunni article of predestination due to the Shiᶜa disagreement with the succession after the death of the Prophet and the denial of the descendants of ᶜAlī their perceived rightful authority to rule the Muslim community. This Shiᶜa affiliation explains why both Ibn Miskawayh and Ṭūsī devoted long sections of their ethics to the subject of justice. Ṭūsī's approach utilises philosophical and mathematical language to define justice, using concepts such as unicity, equilibrium, equivalence and numerical-

1 Ibid., p. 94.

geometrical relationships. Later in the *Akhlāq-i Nāṣirī*, in his chapter on politics, Ṭūsī builds on his understanding of justice as it is in justice that ethics and politics overlap.

According to Ṭūsī, the term 'justice' means equilibrium (*musāwāt*). Equilibrium is the closest state to unicity (*waḥdat*), that is, 'the highest degree of superiority and perfection' as it proceeds from God as the only truly one. In fact, 'equilibrium is the umbra of unicity…and were it not for equilibrium, the circle of existence would not be complete.'[1] Clearly, Ṭūsī is trying to define justice within a metaphysical context with unicity and equilibrium as the pivots of existence. If virtue is acting in accordance with the mean between two extremes—an Aristotelian rule that Ṭūsī follows—and if justice as equilibrium is this mean, as Ṭūsī clearly mentions, then justice is the supreme virtue.

After defining justice, Ṭūsī employs two types of relations among numbers—continuous (*muttaṣil*), where the relation of 2 to 4 is like 4 to 6, and discrete (*munfaṣil*), where the relation of 2 to 4 is like that of 6 to 8—to explain three areas for the application of justice in daily life: 1) in possessions and favours; 2) in transactions and exchanges; 3) in corrections and penalties.[2] These three areas are identical with what we know today as property rights, transaction rights and legal rights.

In the first application, justice is served if some property or favour is secured equally to two people when the relation of one of them to that property is the same as the relation of the other one to that property. The relationship here is mathematically discrete. In the second application, where it is a matter of transactions or exchanges, the relations can be either continuous or discrete. For example,

1 Ibid., p. 95.
2 Ibid., p. 96.

in a continuous relation, the relation of this cloth to this gold is as that of this gold to this bench so one can justly exchange the bench for the cloth. In a discrete relation, the relation of this draper to this cloth is that of this carpenter to this bench and so the cloth and the bench can be exchanged with no inequity.[1] The third application concerns recompense when some harm is done to someone and the just law compensates the victim proportionately. Here, Ṭūsī characterizes the just person as someone who 'gives proportion and equilibrium to disproportionate and unequivalent things.' He also states that the divine decree is 'the determiner of the mean in every case...[and] the positor of equality and justice.'[2]

It is interesting to note that both Ibn Miskawayh and Ṭūsī introduce money in the context of discussing justice as equilibrium and proportionate division. Money is defined as an essential component of civic life, which revolves around the exchange of commodities and labour between citizens. Money is a medium of compensation and preserving equity. Ṭūsī explains that the three conditions for preserving justice between human beings are the divine commandment, a human arbiter (*ḥākim*) and money. The divine decree is embodied as the religious law (*Sharīʿa*), the human arbiter is primarily a messenger of God, and, finally, there is money. Here,[3] Ṭūsī quotes the verse from the Qur'an that mentions all three conditions: 'We sent our messengers with clear signs, the Scripture and the Balance, so that people could uphold justice: We also sent iron, with its mighty strength and many uses for mankind...'[4] It is at this point in the dis-

1 Ibid.
2 Ibid., p. 97.
3 Ibid., p. 98.
4 Q. LVII.25.

cussion that justice is contrasted with its opposite, injustice or tyranny (*jawr*). The worst kind of injustice is exerted when a person or a society defies the divine law, medial injustice consists of disobeying the human arbiter, and the lowest form of injustice occurs when monetary laws are broken.[1] Ṭūsī here emphasizes that these injustices can ruin civic prosperity and he concludes with lengthy passages on the views of philosophers on justice mostly attributed to Aristotle and Ibn Sīnā.

How to Become Virtuous

In the *Akhlāq-i Nāṣirī*, the above discussion on the superiority of the virtue of justice is followed by a discussion on the acquisition of virtue. The two key terms Ṭūsī uses here are 'nature' (*ṭabīʿat*) and 'craft' (*ṣināʿat*). Wickens has translated the second term as 'discipline' due to its regulatory function in relation to our natural faculties. The argument put forth is that no one is born virtuous and 'virtue is a matter of discipline' and habit formation. Thus, ethics can be said to be similar to medicine and Ṭūsī refers to it as 'spiritual medicine.' If ethics is considered from this angle, then one needs to examine the different faculties of the soul to see if each possesses equilibrium. If it does not, then discipline and correction are required to perfect the faculty.[2] So, to be virtuous one needs to preserve the health of the soul and prevent its sickening. One way to preserve spiritual health is to keep the company of good people and avoid that of vicious ones. Another way is to form a habit of doing good things consistent with both theoretical and practical wisdom. Thus, reflection and avoidance of indulgence in material pleasures can help the soul attain

1 Ibid.
2 Ibid., pp. 111–112.

the state of virtue. Studying and practising philosophy is an example of the former, and self-control is an example of the latter.[1]

As for vice, it is considered a treatable disease of the soul. Just like diseases of the body, vices result from a loss of equilibrium either through excess or through deficiency. For example, an excessive application of the rational faculty would be extreme speculation and judging abstract entities in the same way as sensible objects. An example of a deficient application of the rational faculty is to stop short of certainty and to be satisfied with sophistry and divination.[2]

To know how to cure vicious traits and habits, one needs to look into their causes and, once they are identified, to remove them. It is interesting that Ṭūsī considers immorality as a disease that can be treated. Nobody acts immorally by nature and vices in one's character are the result of some psychical conditions that can be caused by bodily defects. He elaborates on different stages and forms of cure and says that only when all cures have proved ineffective can one resort to mortifying force and punishment; this is comparable with surgery which is prescribed when other treatments do not work.[3]

Ṭūsī categorizes psychical diseases that cause immoral traits in accordance with the division of the human soul into rational, irascible and appetitive. He lists several diseases along with their specific cures under each faculty. For example, remaining ignorant without an attempt to remove ignorance is one of the diseases of the rational soul. Arrogance is one of the diseases of the irascible fac-

1 Ibid., pp. 115–120.
2 Ibid., p. 123.
3 Ibid., pp. 124–125.

ulty, and idleness is a disease of the appetitive faculty. Among the vices that Ṭūsī lists are some that are not commonly considered as vices. For example, the fear of death, which is discussed at length, is regarded as a vice. The cure for the fear of death is similar to that which Ṭūsī applies to many of the other diseases he lists. This prescribed cure is the acquisition of true knowledge and insight. In the case of the fear of death, one needs to investigate the meaning and nature of death.[1] Although Ṭūsī does not discuss the Ismaʿili doctrine of instruction in this context, the emphasis on learning and recognition implies the necessity of a guide who can help people see the true nature of their vices. In light of the medical analogy that he uses throughout these passages, one can compare this guide, who in the Ismaʿili context is the imam or his representative, to a healer of the soul.

Economics

The chapter on economics in *Akhlāq-i Nāṣirī* is half as long as the chapter on ethics and is independent of Ibn Miskawayh's book on ethics, which does not discuss economics at all. Apart from Greek sources, Ṭūsī's understanding of economics is influenced by Ibn Sīnā's *Kitāb al-siyāsa* (The Book of Politics). Following Aristotle's categorization of practical wisdom, Ṭūsī understands economics as the management of the household (*tadbīr-i manzil*) and this includes possessions and properties, family and servants. The key to family welfare is equilibrium. In accordance with the patriarchal milieu of the time, the addressee of the passages in this part of the book is the man as head of the household. Ṭūsī's patriarchal perspective is particularly obvious in the contemptuous manner

1 Ibid., pp. 126–149.

of describing women as less intelligent and more prone than men to evil deeds such as jealousy, sloth and idleness.[1] Ṭūsī's tone in this regard is more aligned with gender hierarchy in the Greek context than in the Qur'anic discourse, according to which men and women are equal at the ethical level.

After elucidating the necessity of the family for the survival of the human species and enumerating the components that constitute a household, Ṭūsī states that as an organization of plural elements a household 'demands a kind of unity' that must reside in the 'master of the house', whose role is compared to that of a physician with the responsibility to preserve the health of the family.[2] The welfare of the family is guaranteed if the head of the family keeps the necessary balance in property and provision, in the regulation of the wife or wives, in the management of children and in the governance of servants. Among these categories of household management, it is only the first one that fits into our modern understanding of economics. But for Ṭūsī, economics is about the unity that results from an intelligent and balanced management in all the four above domains.

An intelligent management of property and provision involves income, custody and expenditure. A healthy income is one that is earned justly. Here, justice involves the person himself and others in the sense that one should not earn money by means of injustice towards others and neither should one earn it by abasing oneself. It is also important that the means of income be a noble one. According to Ṭūsī, one should not earn money by means of a base craft such as sorcery when one can earn it by a means that is more noble. For him, noble crafts are those of 'the men of culture and

1 Ibid., p. 165.
2 Ibid., pp. 154–156.

letters', and also of those active in politics and the military. There are also some intermediate crafts such as agriculture and carpentry.[1] Ṭūsī's hierarchical classification of crafts falls into the category of political economy and resonates with Plato's utopian republic and Fārābī's perfect state, as well as the pre-Islamic Persian society.[2]

As for custody and expenditure, it is concerned with the balance between income and expenditure, as well as the objects of expenditure. Ṭūsī gives a list of conditions whose fulfilment would guarantee steady and legal wealth. In speaking about the objects and manner of expenditure, Ṭūsī's economic discourse includes the concept of righteousness. For example, charitable giving with a light heart, no regrets, and no expectation of gratitude or fame can gain the person proximity to God.[3]

The section on the regulation of wives is all about control and the exertion of male authority on a 'lesser' gender; Ṭūsī regards women as lesser human beings without agency. Women are not the objects of love or even lust. Rather, the twofold motive for marrying a woman is 'the preservation of property and the quest for progeny.'[4] If the man is not wise enough to keep his wife under his control, she may become a 'despot' and ruin the family.[5] On this topic, one would expect to see Ṭūsī make some exceptions given the Muslim traditions that revere women, especially those in the Prophet's family. But in this work, he simply talks about women in general with no exceptions.

1 Ibid., pp. 157–158.
2 For more on this topic, see Antony Black, *The History of Islamic Political Thought from the Prophet to the Present*, Edinburgh: Edinburgh University Press, 2011, pp. 155–156.
3 Ṭūsī, *The Nasirean Ethics*, p. 160.
4 Ibid., p. 161.
5 Ibid., pp. 164–165.

The longest section of Ṭūsī's discussion of household management focuses on the management of children by whom he primarily means male children. Female children are totally ignored and all the instructions address boys only. There is much emphasis on discipline, piety and education. From early childhood, one must teach the child submission to rules. One of the first things that he must be taught is to avoid the company of ignoble characters and to form the habit of mingling with noble ones so he can form a love of nobility. Here, Ṭūsī notes that nobility is gained by 'intelligence, discrimination and piety, and is not dependent on property and race.'[1] The removal of race and wealth as factors in creating social hierarchy can be regarded as some progress in comparison to his stratification of society in the beginning of this part of the book, which followed the Greek model of social hierarchy. The inclusion of piety here brings Ṭūsī closer to the Qur'anic idea of nobility, namely, piety. In fact, piety has a very wide scope in Ṭūsī's discourse on childhood education. It includes a considerable range of restrictions on what a male child wears, how he looks, what he eats, says, listens to and reads. In an obviously Platonic tone, Ṭūsī advises the educator to control the genre of poetry children read as certain types of poetry are corruptors of youth; at the top of the list are odes of love and wine-bibbing. The poetry Ṭūsī recommends is poetry that instigates valour.[2] In this context, Ṭūsī specifies that the tutor of children must be selected with care. He should be an intelligent and faithful person with charisma and 'manliness'. He should also be a person of good reputation who can communicate with all classes of people. He should be fair towards all pupils and if it is necessary to punish them,

1 Ibid., p. 167.
2 Ibid., p. 168.

then do so in a mild manner. Children must choose those crafts that best suit their talents and potential.

The section on the management of children ends with a few passages on parental rights. Ṭūsī informs us that this part was added to the second edition of *Akhlāq-i Nāṣirī*, which he revised about thirty years after completing the first edition. Parental rights exist because parents are the intermediary cause in the creation of children and because they provide for their material and spiritual needs. There is a difference between the rights of the mother and those of the father. Maternal rights are physical and this is why children, as soon as they can have sensations, recognize their mothers. But the rights of the father are spiritual, so the child comes to recognise his father only upon reaching intellectual maturity. The child is expected to show his parents sincere love, assistance when required, benevolence both in private and public regarding all matters of this world and the next, and avoid all kinds of disrespect and disobedience. These are among the virtues that one can form with regard to parents.[1]

The section on the regulation of servants is very short. Ṭūsī begins with the necessity for the existence of servants and calls them 'pledges from Almighty God' to whom the employer must show benevolence, gentleness and encouragement. Yet Ṭūsī clearly considers servants to possess a lower level of intelligence and this can be seen in his explanation of the ways in which they should be encouraged and disciplined. At best servants are regarded as children, and at worst as beasts. The most shocking part of this section is where Ṭūsī advises people to put slaves at their service instead of ordinary servants.[2] This is far from

1 Ibid., pp. 178–180.
2 Ibid., pp. 181–184.

the approach of the Prophet Muḥammad towards slavery; he always recommended the freeing of slaves as a virtuous act. This again is one of those subjects that Ṭūsī comments on from a Greco-Roman perspective rather than an Islamic one. Ṭūsī ends the section on the regulation of servants by commenting on the serving aptitudes of different ethnic groups including Arabs, Persians, Indians, Turks and Romans. It is interesting to note that Ṭūsī makes no comments on the serving capacity of Mongols, who were his lords at the time he added the section on the regulation of servants!

Politics

The third and last part of *Akhlāq-i Nāṣirī* is on politics and, as Ṭūsī acknowledges at the beginning of this part, it relies largely on the teachings of Abū Naṣr Fārābī.[1] However, Ṭūsī's political discourse also includes strong Shiʿa and Persian elements, especially in his narratives of the imamate and kingship.

Ṭūsī begins his discussion of politics with the Aristotelian idea of the interdependence of humanity and civic community. Human virtues can flourish only when individuals mingle and cooperate with each other. The perfection of humanity is not possible outside a social network as 'no individual can reach perfection in isolation.'[2] Social life is a combination of different crafts, opinions, demands and purposes. To maintain a balance of power between people and preserve their rights, a society requires a form of management which is known as government. Pivotal to any government is justice in the sense of equilibrium of rights. But the need for justice, which is called 'an artificial union', is the result of the

1 Ibid., p. 187.
2 Ibid., p. 195.

absence of love, which is 'a natural union'.[1] As opposed to Ibn Miskawayh, who discusses love only under ethics, for Ṭūsī the link between love and justice and the importance of love in human relationships explain why he dedicates one whole section of his politics to love. Similarly, the virtue of friendship, which is discussed only under ethics by Ibn Miskawayh, appears under politics in Ṭūsī's work. Ṭūsī's discussion of politics also includes sections on social virtues, different types of authority, different forms of governments and cities, and the role of the Shiʿa imams.

Love

After briefly reviewing the metaphysical narrative of love in Greek philosophy, including love in the philosophy of Empedocles, where it is regarded as the cause of order and unity for all existents, Ṭūsī turns his attention to love between human beings. Love is the reason why humans come together as a society. He believes that love per se can only happen between rational beings and that humans are by nature prone to it. It is a kind of force that can unify people and societies. The Arabic-Persian term Ṭūsī uses for love is '*maḥabbat*', and this applies to all kinds of affection which can have different motivations. The main divisions of love are based on origins and ends. In origin, love can be natural or voluntary. Natural love is best exemplified by a mother's love for her child. As for voluntary love, Ṭūsī comes up with different categories: love that is quick to form and quick to end; love that is quick to form and slow to end; and love that is slow to form and slow to end. As for the ends of love, they can be pleasure, profit, the good or a combination of all these.

1 Ibid., p. 196.

In voluntary love, which is the main topic of the section, what is motivated by pleasure alone is generally quick to form and quick to disappear. Ṭūsī's example of a pleasure-motivated love is love between young men. Another example of this kind of love would be what is caused by mere sexual attraction and would disappear as soon as the relationship is consummated. Profit is usually the cause of that kind of voluntary love, which grows slowly but ends quickly as soon as the profit is gained. For Ṭūsī, the strongest and most enduring form of love is motivated by the good (*khayr*) and develops between good people. This kind of love is quick to grow 'by virtue of the essential affinities between men of good, [and it is] slowly dissolved because of the true union necessary to the nature of good, which renders dislocation impossible.'[1]

Among the different types of love, only the love between good people and which is for the sake of the good is untainted by transience and imperfections. Before expounding on love between good people, Ṭūsī mentions the ultimate form of pure love, which is caused by the 'divine substance' of human beings. This type of love is claimed for those who 'assimilate themselves to God' (*muta'allihīn*), and Ṭūsī makes sure to limit it to rare cases and exclude many 'pretenders'.[2] Ṭūsī must have intended true mystics (*ʿurafā*), and his knowledge of Sufism and his conversations with some of the Sufis of his time would have influenced him here. Ṭūsī's use of such terms as the 'illumination of the presence' (*ishrāq-i ḥuḍūr*) and 'effusion' (*fayḍ*) in reference to the relation between the mystic and God also point to Sufi influences. Yet in this passage, he makes no reference to Sufism and only mentions Aristotle,

1 Ibid., p. 197.
2 Ibid., p. 198.

citing Heraclitus in the *Nicomachean Ethics*, on the attraction between things of a similar nature, implying that proximity to God guarantees a perfect or divine love.

As for love between good people, Ṭūsī believes that both reason and revelation invite us to it. This love is pure of the imperfections of both pleasure-driven and profit-driven love. Ṭūsī states that a reason why the religious law (*Sharīʿa*) recommends that some of our religious duties—such as the communal prayer or the pilgrimage to Mecca—be performed communally is that by nature communal activities create unity. Ṭūsī believes the sense of fellowship that is created during communal rituals can grow into love.[1]

Pure love between good people that is motivated by a quest for virtue, and that Ṭūsī considers a rarity, is not to be found among the masses. The result of this love is 'mutual good council and justice of transaction'. For example, a father's love for his child is motivated by the fact that he sees the child as his 'second self' and so wishes for him all the virtues that he may either possess or that he strives for. Ṭūsī finally states that the love of a virtuous ruler for his people is similar to paternal love and that a ruler should relate to his subjects in the manner of a sympathetic father who enjoins good and prohibits evil.[2]

Cities of Virtue and Cities of Vice

As mentioned above, Ṭūsī's politics are deeply influenced by Fārābī. Ṭūsī's fundamental division of societies or cities is into virtuous and unvirtuous ones. There is only one kind of virtuous city but there are many types of unvirtuous ones. The difference between a virtuous city and all the

1 Ibid., p. 200.
2 Ibid., pp. 202–203.

unvirtuous ones is the latter's deviance from rationality; cities can go astray in multiple ways because there are multiple ways of being irrational and erroneous.[1]

Ṭūsī's passages on the virtuous city in *Akhlāq-i Nāṣirī* are an interesting complex of Platonic epistemology and politics, Fārābī's adaptation of Plato's *Republic*, Peripatetic psychology, Ismaʿili narratives of divine inspiration and authority, as well as Persian theories of kingship. According to Ṭūsī, one of the keys to the formation and subsistence of a virtuous city is agreement or harmony among the citizens in both opinions and actions. As for opinions, the citizens should agree on the beginning and the end, that is, the origin of humanity and its final end, as well as agreeing on the state between the two in this world. This requires a shared philosophical and religious ideology between the citizens. Agreement in actions is achieved when the citizens are guided by reason and justice. Therefore, right action is preceded by right opinion that derives from wisdom. However, societies consist of people with different intellectual capacities. Ṭūsī regards this as a natural cause of social order, or social stratification and the hierarchical distribution of power. Following the example of Plato and Fārābī, Ṭūsī considers authority to be dependent on knowledge; this true knowledge is not equally available to all people. In identifying the possessors of true knowledge, Ṭūsī incorporates Fārābī's Islamic Prophetic narrative while maintaining the Platonic legacy by attributing the highest rank of wisdom to philosophers. The Ismaʿili discursive influence on Ṭūsī's theory of authority can be seen in his attribution of divine inspiration (*ta'yīd-i ilāhī*) to the possessors of true knowledge of

1 Ibid., p. 211.

the beginning and end of humanity.[1] This is the epithet that Ṭūsī frequently uses in his Ismaʿili writings in reference to the Shiʿa imams and their representative, or *ḥujja*.

In a later passage, Ṭūsī refers to the ancient Persian king and founder of the Sassanid empire, Ardishīr Bābakān, calling him an 'Iranian philosopher', which shows his high regard for Ardishīr as a perfect ruler. It is interesting to note here that for Ṭūsī a virtuous society is not necessarily an Islamic one, though he regards the existence of a religion as a necessity in a virtuous city. Ṭūsī quotes Ardishīr Bābakān saying that 'religion and kingship' are twins. Given that the religion of the Sassanid era was Zoroastrianism, one can say that, at least in the context of politics, Ṭūsī agrees with Fārābī on the symbolic character of religions as representations of the same truth.[2] This is also in harmony with Ṭūsī's belief in the Ismaʿili distinction between the esoteric and exoteric.

For Ṭūsī, social stratification is based on the possession of knowledge. Thus, the highest social level in a city should be the possession of philosophers because their knowledge of the origin, purpose and current state of humanity is 'sheer intellectual knowledge' removed from imaginative and corporeal forms. One level below them is that of 'the people of faith' (*ahl-i īmān*), whose knowledge is based on estimation. Here, Ṭūsī is returning to the Avicennan division of the rational faculty into intellection, estimation, imagination and sense perception. The knowledge of the people of faith is at the level of estimation, which allows them to grasp particular meanings without being attached to corporeal forms. What makes this group of people superior to the group below them is that they admit philosophical knowledge is superior to their own knowledge. The next level is that of the 'people of assent'

1 Ibid., p. 212.

2 Fārābī, *Mabādi' ārā' ahl al-madīna al-fāḍila*, pp. 277–285.

(*ahl-i taslīm*). While limited to imagination and corporeal knowledge, these people also acknowledge their own imperfection and affirm the knowledge of the previous groups as being closer to the truth. The lowest level is that of 'the negligible' ones (*mustaḍʿafān*); they do not possess any knowledge apart from some fixed images and they are not aware that their knowledge is far removed from the truth. By calling this group of people 'image-worshippers' (*ṣūrat-parastān*),[1] Ṭūsī's narrative becomes reminiscent of the chained prisoners in Plato's cave analogy who take for real the shadows on the wall. This group can also be identified as the exoterists (*ahl-i ẓāhir*) in Ismaʿili parlance, meaning those people who are only fixed on the outer aspects of the religion. This idea also appears in *Rawḍa-yi taslīm*, in a section entitled 'On Refinement of Character' (*tahdhīb al-akhlāq*), a title that is identical to that of Ibn Miskawayh's book. In this section, people are categorized as follows: 'People of the realm of physical senses' (*ahl-i kawn-i maḥsūs-i jismānī*), 'denizens of the realm of spiritual imagination [or spiritual estimation]' (*ahl-i kawn-i mawhūm-i rūḥānī*) and 'people of the realm of intelligible existence' (*ahl-i kawn-i mawjūd-i ʿaqlānī*).[2] There is a partial correspondence between these types of people and those quoted above from *Akhlāq-i Nāṣirī*.

After explaining the levels of people in a virtuous city, Ṭūsī focuses on one of the key ideas in his politics, namely, the perfect ruler. The role of the ruler is to guarantee harmony and the attainment of communal happiness for all levels of society. He 'settles each group in its own place and location, and organizes authority and service among them.' The ruler—who is also referred to as 'the legislator' and 'head of the city'—resembles the rational faculty in regulat-

1 Ṭūsī, *The Nasirean Ethics*, pp. 212–213.
2 Ṭūsī, *Paradise of Submission*, p. 108.

ing the faculties of the soul. For Ṭūsī, 'the legislator' can be a prophet because he assigns to the legislator the charge of enacting the law (*Sharīʿa*); this is the ideal legislator. Ṭūsī, then, continues his discourse on leadership and authority by categorizing different levels of authority beginning with the supreme authority of a king. The absolute king (*malik ʿalā'l-iṭlāq*) can easily be identified as a philosopher because his mark is complete intellection and his rule is the rule of wisdom. Ṭūsī's conception of kingship is informed both by Plato's idea of a philosopher-king and the Persian model of a wise monarch, an example for Ṭūsī embodied in Ardishīr Bābakān. The king has four characteristics, namely, wisdom (*ḥikmat*), complete intellection (*taʿaqqul-i tāmm*), power of persuasion and imagination, and power of defence and protection. In the absence of such an individual, authority devolves to a council made up of several individuals. The best council is that of 'the most virtuous ones' (*afāḍil*) who collectively possess the four qualities of the king. In the absence of such a council, authority devolves to an individual who has knowledge of the traditions (*sunan*) of the previous rulers and has the ability to enact them and to unify his people under these traditions. In the absence of such an individual, authority devolves to a group of people who can together do the same job. The last two categories of authority must also possess the power to persuade people towards perfection and to protect them from evil.[1]

Moving on to unvirtuous cities, and still modelling his ideas on those of Fārābī, Ṭūsī identifies several kinds of unvirtuous cities. 'Ignorant cities' are those that lack knowledge; their ethical imperfections are due to the ignorance of their inhabitants. 'Impious cities' are those whose inhabitants have

1 Ṭūsī, *The Nasirean Ethics*, pp. 214–217.

knowledge of what is good but act otherwise. And 'errant cities' are those whose inhabitants have mistaken a representation of real happiness for the real happiness itself.

Each of these three unvirtuous cities are divided into several types. Ṭūsī details six types of ignorant cities, which he also refers to as a model for the divisions of the impious and errant cities; the number of impious and errant cities is said to be unlimited.[1] But, while the causes of their deviation from the good and from happiness are different, the ways in which they act unethically are similar and roughly amount to six.

'The necessary city' is an assembly (*ijtimāʿ*)[2] of people who work together for the purpose of maintaining their basic bodily needs such as food and clothing. They use different mediums for fulfilling their needs, that is, a variety of crafts among which some may rank higher than others, or they simply may use one mode of livelihood such as agriculture. The most virtuous among the inhabitants plays the role of their chief and uses people as his labour force.[3] Ṭūsī seems to use the term 'virtuous' here in the very broad sense of being capable and skilful.

'The servile city' is an 'assembly of wickedness' (*ijtimāʿ-i nadhālat*) whose inhabitants amass wealth beyond necessity. They do this by different means such as commerce, agriculture, hunting or even stealing from travellers or other cities. The head of such a city is the one who is best at finding ways of acquiring wealth and treasuring it.

'The base city' is an 'assembly of meanness' (*ijtimāʿ-i khissat*) whose inhabitants only seek bodily pleasures and overindul-

1 Ibid., p. 225.
2 Wickens has translated *ijtimāʿ* as 'combination', but 'assembly' is a better equivalent for the Arabic term in this context.
3 Ibid., p. 218.

gence in worldly ones. Such a city is led by a person who is proficient in the techniques of entertainment and who helps his people achieve the greatest indulgence in bodily pleasures.[1]

'The city of noble status' is discussed in greater detail than the previous types of ignorant cities. This city is an assembly of people who seek noble status (*karāmat*) in words and deeds. This may at first glance sound like a virtue, but in effect the manner in which this noble status is achieved is not itself noble. Ṭūsī pictures noble status in an ignorant city as either a traded property between citizens of the same or other cities, or as domination (*ghalaba*) of one city by another, or as lineage (*ḥasab*). Moreover, affluence here plays an important role in the attainment and preservation of noble status. The head of this city is a man who has lasting fame as well as wealth. If the citizens are assigned their due levels and the desire for ennoblement is kept within balance, this city could be the best among unvirtuous cities. Otherwise, excessive identification with noble status can turn this city into a despotic regime or the 'city of domination'.[2] Ṭūsī's description of the city of noble status is best understood against the background of timocracy in Plato's classification of cities, as well as an appreciation of the idea of aristocracy in Arab and Persian societies.

The 'city of domination' (*taghallub*) is an assembly of people whose main desire is to take possession of other people's lands, money or lives. Management of such a city is based on fighting, bloodshed, slavery, fraud, treachery and the humiliation of others. The citizens of such a city may be compelled to participate in such vicious acts by the head of the city, who is a conqueror. Also, the city may be home to oppressed minorities whose lands and possessions

1 Ibid.
2 Ibid., pp. 220–221.

have been taken from them by the conqueror. Regarding the city of domination, Ṭūsī divides it into different types in accordance with the purpose of its inhabitants, which may be a combination of conquest with pleasure, nobility, wealth or other such motives.[1] Although Ṭūsī does not give any examples of the city of domination apart from a passing reference to Pre-Islamic Arabia, it is possible that he may have had the Mongols in mind as at the time of writing the first edition of *Akhlāq-i Nāṣirī* he had taken refuge from the Mongols in the Ismaʿili fortress.

The last type of unvirtuous city is the 'city of the community', one that is built on an 'assembly of freedom' (*ijtimāʿ-i ḥurriyyat*). This is the closest to Fārābī's idea of democracy (*al-madina al-jāmiʿiyya*) and Ṭūsī's descriptions of this city are very similar to those of Fārābī. Ṭūsī emphasizes the diversity of races and ethnicities in this city, and the smooth integration of immigrant minorities into the city due to the equality of all residents. He also emphasizes the possibility of the emergence of virtuous traits and characters in the citizens of the city. He says that 'after a passage of time, there appears virtuous and wise men, poets and orators and every one of the many classes of perfect men who, if collected, may be components of the virtuous city.' Yet, just like in other unvirtuous cities, a virtuous person cannot safely rule in 'a city of the community'. Ṭūsī considers this city as the best among the ignorant cities and, unlike Plato, does not overemphasize its tendency to become an anarchy.[2]

At the end of his divisions of unvirtuous cities and before moving on to discuss forms of government, Ṭūsī gives a list of imperfections that can grow within a virtuous state.

1 Ibid., pp. 222–223.
2 Ibid., pp. 224–225.

On the Kingly Rule

Having identified virtuous and unvirtuous cities, Ṭūsī now focuses in particular on the conditions for and the characteristics of the ruler of a virtuous city. Following Plato and Fārābī, Ṭūsī places significant emphasis on the ruler, who is the focal point of social welfare and happiness in a virtuous city. Ṭūsī refers to this ruler as a 'king'; that is understandable if we consider the Greek and Persian background of his political discourse. Yet, at the very beginning of this section, Ṭūsī also refers to the virtuous city/state as 'the imamate'. This is not surprising given his adherence to Shiʿism and the fact that he wrote *Akhlāq-i Nāṣirī* under the patronage of the Ismaʿili imamate. But his mention of the imamate in this context occurs only once, and he immediately moves on to a lengthy discussion of kingly rule. In his *Akhlāq-i Nāṣirī*, the ruler is always referred to as king (*malik* or *pādshāh*) rather than imam or caliph. One would expect that for a Shiʿa thinker like Ṭūsī, the imamate must be the ideal state, but this is not the case in *Akhlāq-i Nāṣirī*. In this context, the significance of the kingly rule could be explained either in terms of both Platonic and Persian influences or as a recommendation for the best form of government during the times when the imam is in concealment. As for the caliph, in this section there is only one anecdote about the Abbasid Caliph al-Ma'mūn, who is only mentioned in an anecdote regarding an eating habit he was resolved to quit. As examples of kings, Ṭūsī mentions the Achaemenid Darius and the Sassanid Ardishīr Bābakān, two kings who are often referred to in Persian history and literature as wise and just rulers.

Before explaining the manners of a king, Ṭūsī characterizes a good kingdom as one with equilibrium between its elements, namely between the social groups that it comprises. The ruler is responsible for preserving the balance of power between these groups by not allowing the domination of one over the others. The first group consists of 'men of the pen', who possess knowledge of different sciences such as law, jurisprudence, geometry, astronomy, medicine and poetry—all these sciences Ṭūsī himself had mastered. The second group is made up of fighters and brave warriors. The third group is comprised of merchants, crafts-people and tax-collectors, and they are in charge of daily financial matters. The last social group includes those who feed the community, such as farmers and ploughmen.[1]

Keeping the balance between these groups of people is the first condition for justice that the king must meet. The second condition for the king's application of justice is to rank his people based on their ethical merits. He should hold dear those who are by nature good and urge those who have ethical potential towards perfecting their souls. As for those who are evil, the king must keep his distance from them and, depending on the degree and substance of their evil deeds, the king should preach, prohibit or discipline them for the purpose of correction. Harsh methods of punishment and incarceration may even be necessary. The king must also observe equity in the distribution of power and possessions among the different groups and he must prevent tyranny. Finally, the king must preserve the well-being of all citizens and compensate them for losses.[2]

Ṭūsī supplements the above conditions of a just king with several other characteristics that can guarantee the well-being, order and safety of the city. Among these, balanced and reasonable kindness, and generosity are very important to keep the bond between the king and his

1 Ṭūsī, *The Nasirean Ethics*, p. 230.
2 Ibid., pp. 231–232.

subjects. Of course, kindness must always be accompanied by awe, otherwise, it may lead to greed in the subjects. In addition, a moderate lifestyle is necessary for the king. For example, he should reduce his leisure time and spend more time fulfilling his duties as ruler. Ṭūsī expresses his disdain for those rulers who indulge themselves in bodily pleasures; he considers pleasure-seeking a cause for disorder and immorality in society. The king must also be discrete with the state's secrets and always be informed about the affairs of the state and of those of any enemies by hiring trustworthy informants. In case of internal or external conflicts, the king's first choice should be to handle the situation in peace without resorting to war. But if war is inevitable, he should have the ability to command strategically without resorting to treachery. Once the war is over, the king must maintain a humane attitude towards the defeated enemy and hostages because 'pardoning when one is able (to do the opposite) is more praiseworthy.'[1]

Ṭūsī's section on kingly manners is followed by a section on the manners of the king's subjects, which he models on and cites from a text by Ibn Muqaffā (d. 759/1299), a Persian thinker and translator who wrote in Arabic. This section advises the citizens to show respect, loyalty, and obedience to the king.

After outlining the manners for citizens, Ṭūsī moves on to a discussion of friendship. As was mentioned above, Ṭūsī regards friendship as a subject under politics because he regards it as a guarantee for social and political unity.

Friendship

Relying heavily on Aristotle, Isocrates and Ibn Miskawayh, Ṭūsī divides his discussion of friendship into three catego-

1 Ibid., pp. 233–236.

ries: the value of friendship, methods for obtaining it, and methods for retaining it. For Ṭūsī, friendship is a key to a healthy and successful society. As he explains it, friendship is more than just observing the rules of relationships (*muʿāshirāt*) between people. It is a human value and is necessary for happiness. It is a joy beyond animal and material pleasures. Yet, due to its elevated nature, true friendship is rare and one cannot expect to have a large number of friends. Since friendship is 'the natural disposition of men's souls', one should seek it regardless of social status, wealth and power. For example, emperors and the poor are alike in their need for friendship.[1] In short, friendship is a virtue and a blessing in human life due to the strong bond it can create between people.

As for the methods for gaining friendship, the first requirement is the ability to discern the quality of friendship in people. In this respect, one needs to be able to distinguish hypocritical and deceptive behaviours from genuine and honest ones. One way to make sure that our choice of a friend is right is to look into the person's background including their upbringing, as well as their treatment of their parents and of other people. For example, a main characteristic of a candidate for friendship must be gratitude towards others. To emphasize the importance of gratitude, Ṭūsī mentions that the term 'blasphemy' (*kufr*) in Arabic means ingratitude.[2] A true friend must also be invested with the capacity for kindness, which is possible only if the person is without arrogance, selfishness and overindulgence in pleasures. While in search of a virtuous friend, one must avoid evaluating the candidates based on minor faults and one must be forgiving. Instead, one must try to correct

1 Ibid., p. 243.
2 Ibid., p. 245.

oneself in one's relations to others because true friendship is based on effort on both sides.

Ṭūsī's advice on how to retain one's friendships is to care for friends, support them in hardship, be kind and show the warmth of our hearts to them. One must also avoid contention especially when it is for the sake of showing off cleverness at the expense of the humiliation of a friend. If one finds it necessary to admonish friends for their own benefit, then one needs to find a lenient way of doing so and to admonish them in private. Like other virtues, the virtue of friendship is built on balance. For instance, while showing your admiration towards friends, one must also avoid excess lest it turn into flattery. Ṭūsī ends the section on friendship by emphasizing the social function of all virtues including the virtue of friendship.[1]

The Imam and his Representative

I am discussing the imamate under politics because it is hardly possible to distinguish between the theological and political aspects of the imamate in Ṭūsī's writings, especially in his Isma^cili works. This is reinforced by the fact that in Isma^cilism, especially the Nizārī branch, the question of who represents the concealed imam is also crucial and provides an area where Twelver and Isma^cili politics overlap.

Notwithstanding the theo-political character of the imam in Ṭūsī's Isma^cili discourse, Ṭūsī's main argument for the necessity of the imam is based on epistemic premises that he borrows from Peripatetic philosophy. For Ṭūsī, knowledge is not possible without an imam who actualizes the potential of the human soul to attain truth. He discusses this topic mainly within the theory of instruction (*ta^clīm*) in both *Sayr wa-sulūk*

1 Ibid., pp. 249–252.

and *Rawḍa-yi taslīm*. I discussed the doctrine of instruction and the epistemic role of the imam above in the section on esoteric and exoteric knowledge. Here, my emphasis will be on the social and political implications of the doctrine of the imamate and the status of the imam's representative.

In his autobiography, *Sayr wa-sulūk*, Ṭūsī identifies the imam of the time with the ruler (*ḥākim*); and the term 'ruler' frequently appears in the text. He not only ascribes to the imam unique and infallible knowledge, but also argues that this knowledge is exclusive to the imam, and claims by any others to this knowledge are mere ignorance and falsehood. This unique and infallible knowledge implies the necessity of absolute submission to the imam's leadership. He compares the relationship of human beings to the imam, or 'the administrator (*mudabbir*) and the ruler (*ḥākim*)', to the relationship of the body to the soul, or the relationship of tools to a craftsman.[1] In the same context, he prohibits true followers of the imam from the exertion of free will against the imam's will. The imam's followers are not to question the words and deeds of the imam even if they may appear different from what is in the tradition because the imam, as the 'the possessor of truth' (*muḥiqq*),[2] can express the same unchangeable truths in different ways according to the circumstances. Here, Ṭūsī's narrative of absolute submission to the will of the imam has a strong Sufi undertone, which is supported by the idea in Sufism of the union of the instructor with the disciple 'when the veil is removed.'[3] The very term *muḥiqq* comes from Sufism and was frequently used by Ibn ᶜArabī, the famous Andalusian mystic

1 Ṭūsī, *Contemplation and Action*, p. 49.

2 Ibid. p. 48. In Badakhchani's translation, the term '*muḥiqq*' is rendered as 'the speaker of truth'.

3 Ibid., pp. 45–46.

and master of Ṣadr al-Dīn Qūnawī.[1] But *muḥiqq* is also an Ismaʿili term that Ṭūsī specifically elaborates on in the context of the knowledge of the imam.[2] The Sufi association, however, cannot be overlooked when the narrative tends towards union between the soul of the imam and his follower. Another term with a Sufi connotation that Ṭūsī uses in referring to the imam is 'the pole' (*quṭb*). In the passage below, Ṭūsī ascribes to the imam of the age (*imām-i zamān*) the highest existential ranks that a human can occupy:

> The sacrosanct Divine Essence (*dhāt-i muqaddas*) has made the Imam—may salutations ensue upon mention of him—the manifestation of the sublime Word (*maẓhar-i kalima-yi aʿlā*), the source of illumination (*manbaʿ-i nūr*), the lamp of divine guidance (*mishkāt-i hidāyat*), the lantern of divine glory (*qandīl-i ʿizzat-i ṣamadiyyat*), the scale of obedience and worship (*mīzān-i ṭāʿat wa-ʿibādat*), and the person who embodies His [God's] knowledge and love (*shakhṣ-i maʿrifat wa-maḥabbat-i khudā*). God has made him the centre of the heavens and the pole (*quṭb*) of the earth so that everything which rotates and is stable thereupon might persist as it is by his grace. The continuity of the world's person and spirit is indissolubly linked to the perpetuation of the Imam's person and spirit. [As has been said in tradition], 'if the earth were devoid of an Imam even for a moment, it would perish with all its inhabitants.'[3]

1 For Ṭūsī's correspondence with Qunawī, see A Sufi Gateway below.
2 For a discussion of the meaning of this term in Ismaʿili literature, see Shafique Virani, *The Ismailis in the Middle Ages: A History of Survival, a Search for Salvation*, Oxford: Oxford University Press, 2007, pp. 174–175.
3 Ṭūsī, *Paradise of Submission*, p. 120. I have made slight modifications to Badakhchani's translation.

The above passage is a synthesis of the Isma῾ili narrative of the imam as a manifestation of a divine reality, of the Sufi narrative of the perfect human (*al-insān al-kāmil*) as the raison d'être of creation and of the Shi῾a narrative of the imam as the guarantor of the world's subsistence in existence. The tradition quoted in the passage is recorded in *al-Kāfī* by Kulaynī and it is widely used by later Shi῾a scholars especially those in whose texts Shi῾a and Sufi narratives merge, such as in the writings of Sayyid Ḥaydar Āmulī (d. 787/1385) and Mullā Ṣadrā Shīrāzī (d. 1045/1640). Thus, in his Isma῾ili writings, Ṭūsī seems to precede Āmulī in formulating the Shi῾a doctrine of the imamate within a Sufi framework though Āmulī's synthesis is more explicit and systematic.

As for the imam's political power, Ṭūsī states that sometimes the imam 'finds it advisable to occupy a throne, or possess dominion, wealth, an army and a great treasury.' He regards such a period as an age of total happiness and prosperity. Ṭūsī's description of an imam in this context matches that of a king, which takes us back to his general high regard for a wise king. While it is possible that the use of royal imagery such as throne and treasury is metaphorical, such usage in relation to the imam proves Ṭūsī's belief in the political power of the imam of the age. This is particularly understandable in light of Isma῾ili history with the line of designated imam-rulers and the Persian context of Nizārī Isma῾ilism.

The significance of the imam's political dominion also raises the question of who would be eligible to represent the imam in his absence or occultation. Ṭūsī's answer to this question in its philosophical formulization is important to both the Nizārī context and to the development of this discourse in the early modern and modern Twelver theo-politics. Earlier, I mentioned the question of the representative of the imam as one area where Isma῾ili and Twelver theo-political discourses overlap. To discuss this overlap, let us begin with Ṭūsī's thoughts on the imam's representative found in some of his Isma῾ili and Twelver texts.

In the early days of Isma῾ili history, a *ḥujja* was the representative of Ismā῾īl, the deceased son of the sixth Shi῾a imam, Ja῾far al-Ṣādiq (d. 148/765). Ismā῾īl was believed by some Shi῾a to be alive but hidden from sight and that he would reappear at some point in the future as the *qā'im* or the Mahdi.[1] This doctrine of *qiyāma* (resurrection) gradually changed and in its Nizārī formulation began to refer to the disclosure of esoteric truths after a period of concealment due to the imam's abstinence from spreading his mission in his own words.[2] In the *Rawḍa*, Ṭūsī explains that during the imam's absence, his vice-regency goes to his supreme *ḥujja*, who is the manifestation of the first intellect. As we remember from Ṭūsī's cosmology, the imam himself is the manifestation of the decree, or word, that creates the first intellect in eternity.

The supreme *ḥujja* receives his knowledge and power through the imam by inspiration, or *ta'yīd*. Although all *ḥujja*s are the same in essence and ranking, they have different functions depending on the age in which they serve. The two major categories that Ṭūsī proposes here represent the exoteric and esoteric functions of the *ḥujja*. The exoteric function of the *ḥujja* is likened to 'the hand

1 See Wilferd Madelung, 'Ismā῾īliyya', in P. Bearman, Th. Bianquis, C. E. Bosworth, et al., eds., *Encyclopaedia of Islam*, 2nd ed. (*EI2*), 12 vols., Leiden: E. J. Brill, 1960-2005.
2 For a short history of the doctrine of *qiyāma*, see S. J. Badakhchani's introduction to *Contemplation and Action*, pp. 8–14.

of might' (*dast-i qudrat*). A *ḥujja* with this function is the 'commander' (*farmāndih*) who must 'organize the affairs of the community.' He rules over the kingdom and destroys all that does not fully succumb to his power. The overwhelming aspect of this leader is likened to fire. The esoteric function of the *ḥujja* consists of instructing people and actualizing knowledge and virtue in the community. Ṭūsī refers to this as 'the tongue of knowledge' (*zabān-i ʿilm*) and it is symbolized by water. Usually these two functions are actualized in two different persons, who must cooperate. The hand of might must seek guidance from the tongue of knowledge, while the tongue of knowledge must obey the rules of the hand of might. Yet sometimes the imam entrusts both duties to the tongue of knowledge and thus unites the exoteric with the esoteric missions.[1] So the political aspect of the mission, which is its exoteric side, is as necessary as the esoteric one.

I shall now turn to Ṭūsī's Twelver texts on the subject of the imam and his representative. To begin, Twelvers believe that their imam is in occultation and will remain so until a short period of time before the Last Judgement. He is the twelfth descendant of ʿAlī b. Abī Ṭālib and Fāṭima, not through Ismāʿīl but through Mūsā al-Kāẓim, the other son of Jaʿfar al-Ṣādiq. This is the original point of divergence between Ismaʿilis and Twelvers. Ṭūsī's discussions of the subject of the imam from a Twelver perspective are best found in his famous *Tajrīd* and in *Risāla fi'l-imāma* (Treatise on the Imamate) both written in Arabic in contrast to his Ismaʿili theological texts that are in Persian.

Ṭūsī's characterization of the imam in both the *Tajrīd* and *Risāla fi'l-imāma* is in agreement with Shiʿa traditions

1 Ṭūsī, *Paradise of Submission*, pp. 131–133.

as found in Kulaynī's *Kitāb al-ḥujja* (The Book of Proof) in *al-Kāfī*. Moreover, most of the imam's characteristics echo the description given by Ṭūsī of the ruler or king in his *Akhlāq-i Nāṣirī*. The imam is considered to be morally infallible, to have perfect knowledge of the 'sciences of the religion (*al-ʿulūm al-dīniyya*) and sciences of the world (*al-ʿulūm al-dunyāwiyya*) such as legal matters (*al-sharʿiyyāt*), politics (*al-siyāsāt*), customs and manners (*al-ādāb*), expulsion of the enemies (*dafʿ al-khuṣūm*), and so forth.'[1] In the *Tajrīd*, the list of characteristics also includes superiority in knowledge of 'science and religion, generosity (*karam*), courage (*shajāʿa*) and all other spiritual and physical virtues.'[2]

Ṭūsī's Twelver works share similar narratives about the necessity of the imam's existence, his divine appointment, his infallibility and his inspired knowledge; his inspired knowledge in Twelver discourse corresponds to the term '*ilhām*' rather than '*ta'yīd*'. The content of these Twelver works are for the most part based on Shiʿa traditions and any philosophical ideas are at best implicit. For example, the Neoplatonic tinge of the cosmic status of the Ismaʿili imam is missing in the *Tajrīd* and *Risāla fi'l-imāma*. While the *Tajrīd* is rich in philosophical content, the sections on the imamate are philosophical only in the sense of using logical proofs for the necessity, superiority and infallibility of the imam.

Both the *Tajrīd* and *Risāla fi'l-imāma* list political leadership—which is always mentioned together with the imam's spiritual guardianship—as one of his main responsibilities. In this way, Ṭūsī brings together religious and worldly affairs under the imam's rule. Ṭūsī ascribes to the imam

1 Naṣīr al-Dīn Ṭūsī, *Risāla fi'l-imāma*, ed. Muḥammad Taqī Dānishpazhūh, Tehran: Tehran University Press, 1335 S.H., p. 21.
2 Ḥillī, *Kashf al-murād*, p. 243.

'general sovereignty (*al-riyāsa al-ʿāmma*) in [matters of] the religion and the world.'[1] The terms '*al-riyāsa*' and '*al-ra'īs*' appear frequently in Fārābī's references to the perfect ruler. In a famous passage from *al-Madīna al-fāḍila*, Fārābī refers to the perfect ruler as 'the sovereign (*al-ra'īs*) over whom no other human being has any sovereignty whatsoever; he is the Imam; he is the sovereign of the excellent nation, and the sovereign of the universal state (*al-ra'īs al-ma'mūra kulihā*).'[2] This statement is preceded by a list of the ruler's intellectual and physical virtues, virtues that are very similar to those in Ṭūsī's texts. I believe there is a strong similarity between Ṭūsī's use of 'general sovereignty' and Fārābī's 'sovereignty of the universal state'. Yet, Ṭūsī's use of the sovereignty narrative is explicitly and emphatically Shiʿa, and his writings clearly support this. For example, there are arguments in both the *Tajrīd* and in *Risāla fi'l-imāma* for the appointment of ʿAlī b. Abī Ṭālib as successor by the Prophet himself and arguments that his descendants—up to the last imam, *al-Mahdī al-qā'im*, who is in occultation (*ghayba*)—should inherit his position.

As opposed to his Ismaʿili texts, Ṭūsī's Twelver texts do not mention any *ḥujja*, or representative, for the imam during his occultation. In this regard, his texts reflect the political situation during the different periods of his life especially under the Mongols when any mention of a representative who would be in charge of the imam's political duties could have been considered as a rival to the Mongol rule. Thus, Ṭūsī's political discourse lent itself to a wider attribution of authority beyond the appointed representative of the imam and in favour of a ruler or king who has the required and, for the most part, secular, qualities for governing his domain.

1 Ṭūsī, *Risāla fi'l-imāma*, p. 15.
2 Fārābī, *Mabādi' ārā' ahl al-madīna al-fāḍila*, p. 247.

A Sufi Gateway

Producing texts on Sufi thought and practice does not necessarily make Ṭūsī a disciple of Sufism. Ṭūsī's social and political life makes it hard to claim an allegiance to Sufism for him with any confidence. Just as Ibn Sīnā did, Ṭūsī wrote on all subjects that encompass theoretical and practical wisdom, including Sufism. From Ṭūsī's perspective, Sufism comes under practical wisdom, and his main treatise on Sufism, *Awṣāf al-ashrāf* (Attributes of the Nobles), is on Sufi ethics. In the introduction to this work, Ṭūsī states that the book is a kind of sequel to *Akhlāq-i Nāṣirī*. He explains that while the *Akhlāq* expounds on ethics based on the manners of philosophers, the *Awṣāf* focuses on the way of the saints (*awliyā'*) based on the principles of revelation and reason (*qawāʿid-i samʿī wa-ʿaqlī*).[1] The fact that in his methodology he emphasizes the role of reason is proof that he approaches Sufism from a scholarly point of view rather than as someone who is existentially immersed in it. The rational approach to Sufism adopted in the *Awṣāf al-ashrāf* has been mentioned as a possible reason why—with the exception of some Shiʿa Sufi thinkers such as Sayyid Ḥaydar Āmulī—few Sufis have been attracted to the book.[2] Certainly, this cannot have been the main reason for the book's poor reputation among Sufis. One could speculate that major Sunni Sufis would hardly acknowledge a book written by a Shiʿa theologian and politician as one of their

1 Naṣīr al-Dīn Ṭūsī, *Awṣāf al-ashrāf*, ed. Sayyid Mahdī Shams al-Dīn, Tehran: Sāzmān-i Chāp wa-Intishārāt-i Wizārat-i Farhang wa-Irshād-i Islāmī, 1369 S.H./1990, pp. 6–7.

2 Nasrollah Pourjavady, "ʿIrfān-i Khwāja Naṣīr dar *Awṣāf al-ashrāf*, in N. Pourjavady and Ž. Vesel, eds., *Naṣīr al-Dīn Ṭūsī: Philosophe et Savant du XIIIe Siècle*, Tehran: Institut Français de Recherche en Iran, 2000, pp. 40 & 56.

own since the distribution of texts is normally restrained by material conditions.

Despite his rational approach to Sufism, Ṭūsī's epistemic position is sympathetic towards it and this can be seen in his ranking mystical vision as a form of knowledge higher than philosophical wisdom. For Ṭūsī, true knowledge of God is available only through divine illumination. This unmediated form of knowledge is similar to the 'inspirational knowledge' (*al-ʿilm al-ta'yīdī*) that Ṭūsī ranks as the highest form of knowledge in his Ismaʿili texts. The only difference between the Ismaʿili discourse on inspirational knowledge and the Sufi discourses on illumination is that inspirational knowledge is attributed only to the imams, while in the Sufi discourses the friends of God, or saints (*awliyā'*), who possess this knowledge are not limited to the imams though the imams also occupy the rank of sainthood (*wilāya*).

Aside from the *Awṣāf al-ashrāf*, Ṭūsī's Sufi rhetoric appears in several writings, most importantly *Āghāz wa-anjām*. This is one of his Ismaʿili works that he wrote early in his career. Ṭūsī opens his *Āghāz wa-anjām* with a statement that can be interpreted as one of the main doctrines of Sufism. He says, 'Praise be to the Creator, who is the beginning of all and in whom is the end of all; rather, all is just He.'[1] His reference to all creation as God can be identified as the Sufi doctrine of the 'oneness of being' (*waḥdat al-wujūd*) though he does not use the term itself. Ṭūsī also uses a narrative common in Sufism that expresses loathing for this world and describes it as 'a purgatory' (*barzakh*) between the beginning and the end. He calls it a dark barrier (*sadd-i ẓulamānī*) and describes its inhabitants as sleepwalkers who

1 Naṣīr al-Dīn Ṭūsī, *Origin and Destination*, in S. J. Badakhchani's *Shīʿī Interpretations of Islam*, p. 47.

must die to this world to wake up to a real life.[1] The leitmotif of *Āghāz wa-anjām* is the 'spiritual quest' (*sulūk*) with its two stages of faith (*īmān*) and certainty (*īqān*), both major concepts in Sufism. People of faith (*ahl-i īmān*) believe in what is veiled and in that which they cannot see, while the people of certainty (*ahl-i īqān*) see the truth. Each of these two stages has several levels that resonate with those of the Sufi quest.[2] Most significantly, the *Āghāz* pictures human existence as a descent from heaven and an ascent to it and speaks of the paradise of monotheists (*muwaḥḥidān*) as annihilation (*fanā'*) in God's unity (*tawḥīd*).[3] Ṭūsī returns again to these Sufi concepts of annihilation and 'oneness of being' in another Isma^cili treatise, *Tawallā wa-tabarrā*. Here he states that a man of God is one who desires neither existence nor non-existence, that is, neither this world nor the next, but only God Himself, thus, the one who sees only God and nothing beside Him will be the seeker of unity (*ṭālib-i waḥdat*).[4] The two texts mentioned are replete with Sufi concepts and narratives and the ideas in them are based on the author's interpretation of Qur'anic verses and Prophetic Traditions. Moreover, they follow the methodology of esoteric interpretation (*ta'wīl*) of the Qur'an, which is a common ground between Isma^cilism and Sufism.

Among Ṭūsī's writings with Sufi themes, it is the *Awṣāf al-ashrāf* that has received the most attention from scholars. The original text is in Persian but there is also a famous Arabic translation of it by Rukn al-Dīn Jurjānī, a student of Ḥillī in the eighth/thirteenth century. In the introduction,

1 Ibid., p. 44.
2 Ibid., pp. 57–58.
3 Ibid., p. 52.
4 Naṣīr al-Dīn Ṭūsī, *Solidarity and Dissociation*, in S. J. Badakhchani's *Shī^cī Interpretations of Islam*, pp. 31–32.

Ṭūsī, who was already in his old age when he wrote the book, speaks of his own spiritual potential and how it was not actualized due to obstructions and preoccupations until he was encouraged to pursue the spiritual life by Juwaynī, his fellow scholar working for the Mongols and who he mentions with great honour and respect.[1] The topics covered in *Awṣāf al-ashrāf* revolve around the major theme of Sufim: the path of annihilation and unification in God. The division of subjects in the work is said to be somewhat similar to *Manāzil al-sā'irīn* by Khwāja ʿAbd Allāh Anṣārī (d. 481/1088).[2]

Awṣāf al-ashrāf is divided into six chapters and each chapter contains six sections, except for the last chapter, which contains only one section, namely annihilation (*fanā'*) as the final destination of the Sufi quest. The progression of chapters corresponds to the stages that the soul of the seeker passes through towards the final destination. The first stage is that of faith (*īmān*) and the last is annihilation or 'annihilation in unity', which he takes from his Ismaʿili treatise, *Āghāz wa-anjām*, discussed above.[3] In fact, the spiritual quest detailed in *Awṣāf al-ashrāf* matches that in *Āghāz wa-anjām*.

Ṭūsī starts *Awṣāf al-ashrāf* by explaining the rationale for the structure of the book. He states that the need to set out on the spiritual journey is based on the premise that by self-observation everyone can come to see their imperfections and inherent poverty.[4] This idea is based on the Avicennan premise that there is only one necessary being, which is independent in its existence while everything else is contingent, meaning dependent, in its existence. In

1 Ṭūsī, *Awṣāf al-ashrāf*, p. 7.
2 Pourjavady, 'ʿIrfān-i Khwāja Naṣīr dar *Awṣāf al-ashrāf*', p. 45.
3 Ṭūsī, *Awṣāf al-ashrāf*, p. 9.
4 Ibid., p. 8.

this sense, everything other than necessary being, or God, has an inherent imperfection. This observation creates in people a longing (*shawq*) for perfection (*kamāl*), which urges them to move towards it, hence the necessity for the spiritual journey. Once this point is clarified, Ṭūsī proceeds to expound on the requirements and stations of the journey; there are thirty-one stations in all. Ṭūsī combines the stations under six parts: 1) the beginning of the journey, which includes faith (*īmān*), determination (*thubāt*), intention (*niyyat*), truthfulness (*ṣidq*), mindfulness of God (*inābat*) and sincerity (*ikhlāṣ*); 2) the removal of obstacles, including repentance (*tawba*), asceticism (*zuhd*), poverty (*faqr*), mortification (*riyāḍat*), self-examination and self-observance (*muḥāsabat wa-murāqabat*) and piety for fear of God (*taqwā*); 3) the means of support for the journey, including solitude (*khalwat*), contemplation (*tafakkur*), fear and sorrow (*khawf wa-ḥuzn*), hope (*rajā'*), patience (*ṣabr*) and gratitude towards God (*shukr*); 4) the states that the seeker experiences on the way, including will (*irādat*), longing (*shawq*), love of God (*maḥabat*), knowledge of God (*maʿrifat*), certainty (*yaqīn*) and serenity (*sukūn*); 5) the states experienced at the end of the journey, including confidence in God (*tawakkul*), contentment (*riḍā*), submission (*taslīm*), monotheism (*tawḥīd*), unification (*ittiḥād*) and unity (*waḥdat*); and finally 6) arrival at the destination, which is the annihilation (*fanā'*) of the seeker.[1] So the whole journey is a movement from imperfection towards ultimate perfection through annihilation in the unity of God, and every station is more perfect than the previous one because it is closer to the destination.

Each station under the six parts opens with a verse from the Qur'an and many of them also end with one. There are

1 Ibid., pp. 8–9

also many Qur'anic allusions within the descriptions of the stations. In explaining each of the six parts, Ṭūsī uses philosophical and theological narratives to clarify the meanings of the key concepts. A good example is the section on 'confidence in God' (*tawakkul*), which is the first station of part five. Ṭūsī defines *tawakkul* as confidence in God's providence and the knowledge that His superior wisdom is best for His creation. As for the question of free will in the context of *tawakkul*, Ṭūsī adopts the position of Shiʿa theologians and quotes a tradition that is often attributed to the Shiʿa imam Jaʿfar al-Ṣādiq without mentioning him, on the relation between providence and free will saying, 'it is neither absolute determinism (*jabr*), nor absolute delegation (*tafwīḍ*) [of power to humankind]; but rather a state between the two.'[1] He also describes free will here as one of the intermediary causes of events in the world, and this connects Ibn Sīnā's position on secondary causes to the above Shiʿa interpretation of free will. As for mentioning the Shiʿa imams by name in the book, there is only the fifth Shiʿa imam, Muḥammad al-Bāqir, who is mentioned as an example of someone who has reached the station of 'patience' (*ṣabr*), one of the stages of the spiritual journey under the third part.

Despite the Sufi message of the *Awṣāf al-ashrāf*, the term 'Sufi' does not appear in it and there are no anecdotes about famous Sufis except for two citations in one section of the book, one from Manṣūr Ḥallāj, who is mentioned by name, and another from Bāyazīd Basṭāmī.[2] It is believed that this was the first time that famous Sufis were referred to in an approving manner in Shiʿa literature.[3] By so doing, Ṭūsī seems to have paved the way for later Shiʿa writers to pay

1 Ibid., pp. 70–71.

2 Ibid., pp. 77–78.

3 Pourjavady, 'ʿIrfān-i Khwāja Naṣīr dar *Awṣāf al-ashrāf*', p. 49.

tribute to figures like Ḥallāj and Bāyazīd without fearing disapproval. All told, *Awṣāf al-ashrāf* is a compendium of the Sufi path to God with a style that is intellectually rigorous while also being easy to follow by a layperson.

Before writing *Awṣāf al-ashrāf*, Ṭūsī had entered into correspondence with Ṣadr al-Dīn Qūnawī (d. 673/1274), the well-known disciple of Ibn ʿArabī who was responsible for spreading the teachings of his master among Persians and Turks. In addition to Sufism, Qūnawī was well versed in Peripatetic philosophy, and there was a considerable overlap between his interests and those of Ṭūsī.

The correspondence opens with a short letter in Persian from Qūnawī in which he expresses praise for Ṭūsī by calling him 'the king of all sages' (*malik-i ḥukamā*) and several other honorific epithets that show Ṭūsī's considerable reputation among his contemporaries. Qūnawī gives the reason for his letter as a wish to establish a friendship with Ṭūsī and to benefit from his thoughts.[1] To this letter Qūnawī attached an Arabic treatise, *al-Risāla al-mufṣiḥa* (The Clarifying Treatise), on the inability of human reason to comprehend the 'realities of things' (*ḥaqāʾiq al-ashyāʾ*) in abstraction. In this treatise, he discusses different ranks of knowledge and he places philosophers among those who do not have access to realities. He argues that human reason can only reach the attributes (*awṣāf*) and accidents (*aʿrāḍ*) of things in their delimited existence (*kawnihā mutaʿayyana*).[2] The failure of reason is particularly obvious

1 This letter along with the rest of the correspondence in the original language has been published in Gurdun Schubert, *Annäherungen: Der Mystisch-philosophische Briefwechsel zwischen Ṣadr ud-Dīn Qōnawī und Naṣīr ud-Dīn-i Ṭūsī*, Beirut: Commissioned by Franz Steiner Publishers of Stuttgart, 1995, pp. 11–14.
2 Ibid., p. 40.

in its endeavours to comprehend divine realities and mysteries that can only be reached in the light of 'emanation' (*fayḍ*) and with divine assistance (*imdād*).[1] Accompanying the treatise was a text consisting of his questions about fundamental issues in philosophy, including: the relation between being (*wujūd*) and quiddity (*māhiyya*); the ontological state of quiddities, namely the question of whether they are caused (*majᶜūla*) or not caused (*ghayru majᶜūla*); the nature of the all-encompassing Being (*al-wujūd al-ᶜāmm*); the problems that ensue from the principle of 'from the one issues only one'; and questions about the nature of the human soul and its relation to the body and its fate after the death of the body. For each question, Qūnawī summarizes the answers from the Peripatetic point of view and then proceeds to demonstrate that these answers are not satisfactory.

Ṭūsī's reply to Qūnawī begins with many compliments on the elevated spiritual status of Qūnawī as 'the Pole of all saints' (*quṭb al-awliyā'*) and 'a vice-regent of the prophets' (*khalīfat al-anbiyā'*).[2] Given that the two had never met before, Ṭūsī's use of such terms in addressing Qūnawī must have been due to the far-reaching fame of the latter and the impression that his writings had had on Ṭūsī prior to the correspondence. In his letter, Ṭūsī confirms the receipt of *al-Mufṣiḥa* and the questions. He also acknowledges receipt of another treatise not mentioned by Qūnawī, *Rashḥ al-bāl* (Outpourings of the Mind); this work belongs to the prayer genre and expounds on Sufi experiences and states during the spiritual journey.

In his response to Qūnawī, Ṭūsī displays his own knowledge of the Sufi path and reminds Qūnawī that

1 Ibid., p. 43.
2 Ibid., p. 94.

Rashḥ al-bāl is most beneficial to seekers (*ṭālibīn*) and imperfect novices (*nāqiṣān*).[1] Although Ṭūsī includes himself among those who would benefit from the spiritual content of the *Rashḥ al-bāl*, this was not meant to be taken literally by Qūnawī. In fact, on receipt of the letter, Qūnawī wrote an excusatory response to Ṭūsī explaining that he should not have been sent the treatise and giving greater details of some of the themes of the work.

Ṭūsī's respect for Qūnawī as an advanced Sufi does not stop him from criticizing him on philosophical questions. Here, Ṭūsī's defence of philosophical teachings in the face of Qūnawī's objections are reminiscent of his earlier endeavours to secure Ibn Sīnā's major philosophical positions against critics such as Rāzī. Just like Rāzī, Qūnawī was well versed in philosophy but sceptical about the capacity of human reason. It is clear that Qūnawī's philosophical questions to Ṭūsī are not real questions but objections to the Peripatetic approach to major philosophical issues. Even after receiving Ṭūsī's response, which contains criticisms and corrections, Qūnawī simply replies that his text was not a final draft and blames the shortcomings on the lack of time and the errors of the scribe.[2] Qūnawī then proceeds to write a new treatise, *al-Hādiya* (The Solace), to defend his understanding of the philosophical issues that he addressed at the beginning of his correspondence with Ṭūsī.

Qūnawī's objections address such a wide scope of problems in Islamic philosophy that they can hardly reflect the nuances of these positions and full interpretations of them. Altogether, Qūnawī's body of 'questions' is an attempt by a dedicated Sufi thinker familiar with the language of Islamic philosophy to criticize philosophy

1 Ibid., pp. 89–93.
2 Ibid., p. 132.

using philosophical terms and to downplay the ability of reason in attaining to truth. Ṭūsī's response shows no inhibitions in demonstrating that Qūnawī's objections are either based on his misunderstanding of philosophical problems, or a misinterpretation of Ibn Sīnā's position. For example, he argues that in speaking of 'being' (*wujūd*) and the problem of its application both to necessary being and contingent beings, Qūnawī does not distinguish between univocal (*muṭawāṭi'*) and ambiguous (*mushakkak*) concepts. Ṭūsī emphasizes that being is an ambiguous concept so its application to different things is by gradation, similar to the application of 'light' to the light of the sun and to candlelight.[1] In addition, Ṭūsī proceeds to prove that Qūnawī has misinterpreted Ibn Sīnā's position on the epistemic confinement of human reason to the properties of things and its incapacity to know their reality.[2] Ṭūsī argues that in the context cited by Qūnawī, 'realities of things' refers to the natures (*ṭabā'iʿ*) of individual physical existents rather than the intelligible (*maʿqūlāt*). He maintains that if we did not comprehend the intelligible reality of the physical body (*jism*), we would not be able to know its properties either; for example, the fact that it is impossible for the physical body to be in two locations at the same time.[3]

To sum up, the correspondence between Ṭūsī and Qunawī holds a significant place in the history of discur-

1 Ibid., pp. 97–98. For Ṭūsī on the ambiguity of being, see Toby Mayer, 'Fakhr al-Dīn Rāzī's Critique of Ibn Sīnā's Argument for the Unity of God in the *Išārāt* and Naṣīr al-Dīn aṭ-Ṭūsī's Defence', in ed. David Reisman, *Before and After Avicenna: Proceedings of the First Conference of the Avicenna Study Group*, Leiden: Brill, 2003, pp. 212-217.
2 Ibid., p. 51.
3 Ibid., p. 101.

sive encounters between philosophy and Sufism. Ṭūsī's responses to Qūnawī prove that regardless of his knowledge of Sufi ideas and his scholarly attempt to provide a compendium of Sufi ethics as shown above, his intellectual priority lay with the philosophy of Ibn Sīnā. The correspondence is possible evidence that Ṭūsī approaches Sufism primarily as a scholar rather than as an engaged follower. Yet this correspondence with Qunawī together with his own writings on Sufi ethics also suggest that Ṭūsī recognized the significance of the Sufi discourses of his time and the importance of conversations between philosophy and Sufism as a means of mutual empowerment between two influential, discursive fields. Moreover, due to his religious status as a celebrated Shiʿa theologian, especially in this later stage of his life as both a Twelver scholar and politician, Ṭūsī's recognition of Sufism was an important step towards a conciliation of Sufism and Shiʿism. This partly explains why he is cited widely in later texts that synthesize Shiʿa and Sufi discourses, texts such as the famous *Jāmiʿ al-asrār* (A Compendium of Mysteries) by Sayyid Ḥaydar Āmulī. For example, Āmulī calls Ṭūsī 'the king of scholars and verifiers' (*sulṭān al-ʿulamā' wa'l-muḥaqqiqīn*) and gives Ṭūsī's belief in the inability of reason to know the Essence of God as evidence of Ṭūsī's adherence to the spiritual path.[1] Āmulī also cites *Awṣāf al-ashrāf* on the necessity of spiritual exercise for the intellective faculty in its unravelling of mysteries such as the relation between providence and free will.[2] *Jāmiʿ al-asrār* was a ground-breaking text that guaranteed the incorporation of speculative discourses of Sufism into Shiʿa texts and

1 Ḥaydar b. ʿAlī Āmulī, *Jāmiʿ al-asrār wa-manbaʿ al-anwār*, eds. Henry Corbin and Othman Yahya, Tehran: Anīstītū-i Īrān va-Faransa, 1969, p. 492.
2 Ibid., p. 150.

intellectual history. That Āmulī—who is acknowledged as an influential conciliator of Sufism and Shiʿism—chose to mention Ṭūsī in *Jāmiʿ al-asrār* is not insignificant.

CHAPTER THREE

On Music and Poetry

It should not come as a surprise that a multifaceted scholar like Ṭūsī would be interested in aesthetics, especially given the high regard with which music and poetry are held in Arabic and Persian cultures. In the mediaeval Islamic tradition, music was usually discussed as a theoretical or mathematical science. But in the works of major philosophers such as Kindī, Fārābī, Ikhwān al-Ṣafā and Ibn Sīnā, the philosophy of music is not confined solely to its mathematical aspects. These philosophers also discuss the origin of music and its effects on audiences, including its psychological, ethical and even therapeutic effects.

There is an untitled short treatise on music in Arabic that several scholars attribute to Ṭūsī.[1] The treatise is only a few pages long and focuses on the theoretical aspects of music rather than its function and effects. Except for a few instances where he modifies the views of his past masters, Ṭūsī's musicology is more or less that of Ibn Sīnā. For example, his division of the science of music into the science of composition (*ta'līf*) of musical notes and the science

1 Mudarris Raḍawī, *Aḥwāl wa-āthār*, p. 570.

of rhythm (*īqāʿ*) is modelled on that of Ibn Sīnā.[1] The rigid style of Ṭūsī's text on music may suggest his mere scholarly interest in music rather than an engagement with it. However, there are also some unverified reports that ascribe the invention of a type of flute to Ṭūsī. Whether or not he really made or even played a musical instrument would be hard to verify, especially as admitting to a partiality for music would not have been appropriate for a mediaeval man of his religious stature. But, given Ṭūsī's adventurous and multifaceted character, his interest in Sufism—which is closely associated with music—and his appreciation of poetry and rhythm, it is quite possible that he actually experimented with music.

As for poetry, Ṭūsī—like many Muslim philosophers—followed Aristotle's tradition by including poetics, or the art of poetry (*fann-i shiʿr*), in his works. Not only did he write about poetry but he also composed poems of his own. His poetics demonstrate his specialized and deep knowledge of the subject, as well as his remarkable literacy in both Arabic and Persian poetry. In his writings, Ṭūsī included a chapter on poetry in his *Tajrīd*; it is the last chapter. In addition, the last chapter of Ṭūsī's most important book on logic, *Asās al-iqtibās*, is on poetics. But Ṭūsī went further by writing an independent treatise on poetics entitled *Miʿyār al-ashʿār* (Standard for Poems) and thus affirmed his agreement with Aristotle in regarding poetry as an important discipline in its own right rather than an addendum to logic. Except for the short preface of *Miʿyār al-ashʿār*, which gives

1 Cited by Dāwūd Iṣfahānīyān & Sāsān Sipanta, 'Risāla-yi az Khwāja Naṣīr al-Dīn Ṭūsī dar ʿilm-i mūsīqī', *Journal of the Faculty of Literature and Humanities at Tehran University*, nos. 138 & 139, 1370 S.H./1991, p. 28. On Ibn Sīnā's musicology, see Fadlou Shehadi, *Philosophies of Music in Medieval Islam*, Leiden: E. J. Brill, 1995, pp. 66–80.

a definition of poetry, the work is dedicated to prosody and rhyming patterns, as well as a comparison of Arabic and Persian poetry regarding metrical measures (*ʿarūḍ*). These chapters are of a very technical nature and show Ṭūsī's deep knowledge and research in this field.

Ṭūsī's high regard for poetry as a phenomenon that goes beyond linguistic techniques appears in his emphasis on poetic content and its influence on the audience. Unlike his predecessor, Ibn Sīnā, who considers rhyme (*qāfiya*) essential to poetry, Ṭūsī argues that poetry is not confined to rhymed verse. In his definition of poetry, Ṭūsī maintains that, except in particular poetic genres, rhyme is only one of the concomitants (*lawāzim*) of the poetic form rather than an essential property of it. He emphasizes this point in both *Asās al-iqtibās* and *Miʿyār al-ashʿār*.[1] However, despite this belief, Ṭūsī dedicates a large portion of his poetics to prosody (patterns of rhythm and sound used in poetry), which shows his great command of the subject. For him, the essence of poetry is in its impact on the imagination (*takhyīl*) and he defines it as, 'the impact of a speech (*sukhan*) on the soul such as expansion (*basṭ*) or contraction (*qabḍ*).' Thus, for Ṭūsī poetry is that which has an impact on an audience and a power to make them feel in certain ways and to act accordingly.[2] This power could be ascribed to speech at large, but Ṭūsī explains that poetic speech is more influential because 'the souls of the majority of people are more obedient to imagination than to assertion (*taṣdīq*) [of a truth].' Ṭūsī explains this influence based on the mimetic

1 See Muʿaẓẓama Iqbālī, *Shiʿr wa-shāʿirī dar āthār-i Khwāja Naṣīr al-Dīn Ṭūsī*, Tehran: Sāzmān-i Chāp wa-Intishār-i Wizārat-i Farhang wa-Irshād-i Islāmī, 1370 S.H./1991, pp. 73–77.

2 Ṭūsī, *Miʿyār al-ashʿār*, ed. Jalīl Tajlīl, Tehran: Nashr-i Jāmī, 1369 S.H./1990, p. 22.

nature of imagination. He argues that mimesis (*muḥākāt*) causes wonder in the soul more than assertion does due to the pleasure it brings to the soul. In this regard, he says:

> Although assertion is similar to imagination in that they are both psychic impressions (*infiʿāl-i nafsānī*), the impression made by assertion is by virtue of affirming a statement due to its correspondence to the external fact. But the impression made by imagination is by way of pleasure and wonder from the speech itself rather than considering any other thing.[1]

Ṭūsī includes imagery, figures of speech and thought, eloquence and rhythm among the poetic components that affect the imagination. He argues that, unlike rhyme, rhythm (*wazn*) is an essential property of poetry and the soul takes pleasure in perceiving it. But the perception of rhythm is based on a kind of taste (*dhawq*) that develops through habit. So different peoples (*umam*) may have different linguistic habits and as a result different tastes in relation to rhythm.[2] Thus, Ṭūsī avoids the rigid standards prevalent in his time and anticipates modern flexibility in producing different poetic forms.[3]

Ṭūsī's own poems are all rhymed and are very traditional in both form and themes. He wrote close to seven hundred lines of poetry of different genres; however, only a few have been recognized as being of high artistic merit. In his poetry, Ṭūsī covers ethical, Sufi, philosophical, and astrological subjects. He also composed verses that address important historical events such as the defeat of the Ismaʿilis

1 Ṭūsī, *Asās al-iqtibās*, vol. 1, p. 423.

2 Ṭūsī, *Miʿyār al-ashʿār*, p. 22.

3 Iqbālī, *Shiʿr wa-shāʿirī dar āthār-i Khwāja Naṣīr al-Dīn Ṭūsī*, p. 78.

by the Mongols and the fall of Baghdad. Below, you can see my translation (lacking the original rhythm and rhyme) of a few lines from Ṭūsī's poems.

A didactic quatrain:

As wisdom rules the world order,
you'd better say little.
As livelihood is predetermined,
you'd better want little.
As the rye would not grow more or
less by your will,
You'd better want little, say little,
and be courteous.[1]

A Sufi quatrain that captures the theme of the unity of being (*waḥdat al-wujūd*):

Truly the First One is the only being;
The rest is all illusion and imagination.
All that comes to your sight but He,
Is the double image of the crossed eyes.[2]

A few lines from a philosophical poem on matter (*mādda*) and form (*ṣūra*) in objects and the bestowal of form on matter by an external metaphysical cause:

Ponder on the state of the wax first
To find properly what you seek.
As long as matter and form are not together
People will not call it [the wax] a candle.
As long as you have it as wax
You know it is nothing but a recipient (*pazīrā*).
The image comes to it by the painter
This is known by all who hearken.[3]

On the impact of planets on human affairs:

1 Poems here are cited from Iqbālī, *Shiʿr wa-shāʿirī dar āthār-i Khwāja Naṣīr al-Dīn Ṭūsī*, p. 121.
2 Ibid., p. 115.
3 Ibid., p. 129.

When the moon and mercury are in symmetry
It is best to visit scholars and men of letters.
To seek what you need and to set out on a journey
To embark on these at this time is better.[1]

Clearly, the variety of subjects in Ṭūsī's poetry matches the disciplines in which he was productive. Despite his command of all the major disciplines of his day, he humbly claims inadequacy in one of his poems:

In the rank (*ṣaf*) of knowledge I galloped a lot,
And among gnostics (*ʿārifān*) I raised my head.
As I took the veil off my heart,
I learned there was nothing that I had learned.[2]

In Persian culture, to be humble is the sign of a great soul, and there are many examples of the above expressions of inadequacy by famous scholars and poets in Persian literature. The content of the above lines resonates with a famous quatrain by the celebrated Sufi poet Abū Saʿīd Abu al-Khayr (d. 967/1049). The quatrain is also reported to have been cited by Ibn Sīnā at the end of his life:

Far and wide though my heart traversed this land
Knew not one hair strand while hair splitting.
Thousands of suns though did shine from my heart
Never did it reach the perfection of a particle.

It may sound ironic to end my discussion of the intellectual achievements of Ṭūsī with the above lines on the imperfection of human knowledge. But if Ibn Sīnā admitted to such an imperfection, so did Ṭūsī. The fact that these medieval scholars traversed far and wide across different subjects of enquiry and did not limit themselves indicates their deep awareness of the vastness and transcendence of knowledge rather than the hubris of the ability to grasp it all.

1 Ibid., p. 110.
2 Ibid., p. 118.

CHAPTER FOUR

Legacy

Over the past eight centuries, Naṣīr al-Dīn Ṭūsī's fame has remained constant in the Persian speaking world. In Iran, everyone has heard his name and, regardless of the scope of their knowledge of Ṭūsī's work, they all take pride in him. Ṭūsī's genius is romanticized by Iranians to the same extent that Leonardo Da Vinci's (d. 1452) is by Italians. The comparison is not far-fetched because both were polymaths who received courtly patronage and had a long-lasting impact on the national consciousness; in Ṭūsī's case, this was also reinforced by his choice to write some of his major works in Persian rather than Arabic. Ṭūsī's importance to Iran is also due to his Shiʿa affiliation and scholarship. Several schools and higher educational institutions across Iran are named after Ṭūsī, among them a highly ranked university of science and technology in Tehran, Khaja Nasir University. Furthermore, his scientific and philosophical works are discussed in many university courses, most importantly in philosophy, logic and history of science programmes.

Aside from his status as an intellectual and national celebrity in Iran, Ṭūsī's scholarly impact on the history of Muslim theoretical and practical wisdom is comparable only to that of Ibn Sīnā, who served as a model for Ṭūsī's scientific and philosophical endeavours. Although Ṭūsī's work in philosophy does not match Ibn Sīnā's in originality, one can still see the same passion, rigour and variety in his writings. Ṭūsī set an inspiring model for the generations that followed him in how to preserve the intellectual legacy of earlier masters through the writing of commentaries on their works and through responses to their critics. As discussed earlier in this volume, Ṭūsī played an important role in defending Ibn Sīnā against his critics while elucidating the master's major philosophical views and expanding on his arguments. Ṭūsī the logician knew how to highlight the nuances of Ibn Sīnā's arguments and based his defence of Ibn Sīnā on the logical inconsistencies of his critics. Yet in doing this, he also developed an art of conversation between scholars. The discursive tradition that Ṭūsī contributed to with his commentaries, critical responses and lengthy correspondences gradually led to the development of a rich tradition of synthesizing various intellectual discourses.

Regarding this synthesizing tradition, one of the places where Ṭūsī's influence is obvious is in the work of Sayyid Ḥaydar Āmulī, who is known for explicating the Shiʿa theory of the imamate within the framework of Ibn ʿArabī's mysticism. In addition to citations from Ṭūsī's works, Āmulī seems to have been inspired by Ṭūsī's synthetic and overall holistic approach. Ṭūsī's innovation in methodology continued through the early modern times, especially in the works of Mullā Ṣadrā, who was a master of mystical philosophy, and who synthesized Peripatetic, Illuminationist and Sufi ideas and arguments. As briefly explained earlier in this work, Mullā Ṣadrā was also deeply influenced by Ṭūsī's eschatology, a fact that he does not acknowledge, most likely because the source that he copied from was one of Ṭūsī's Ismaʿili treatises. Like many of the Shiʿa scholars after Ṭūsī, Mullā Ṣadrā was also indebted to him for his philosophical and mystical approach to theology; this can be found in Mullā Ṣadrā's passages on the imamate in his *Sharḥ uṣūl al-kāfī*.

During his long and eventful career, Ṭūsī produced invaluable texts in almost all the areas of knowledge of the day. He was as interested in the natural world as the human and social domains of religion, ethics, economics, politics and the arts. Some of the works that he produced have set methodological and terminological frameworks for later scholarship, and some were unique in their scope and influence during the medieval ages and even later centuries. Ṭūsī appreciated the power of collective knowledge and scholarship, and he benefited from it throughout his career, beginning with his collaboration with Ismaʿili scholars in his youth and then with the work he did for his Mongol patrons in establishing a scientific centre and library in Marāgha, which in turn created a community of scholars and scientists. The astronomical works produced as a result of Ṭūsī's team leadership are recognized as part of the scientific progress towards the Copernican revolution.

Regardless of his real religious affiliation and despite all the ambiguities surrounding it, Ṭūsī played an important role in shaping philosophical frameworks for both Ismaʿili and Twelver theologies. Ismaʿilis and Twelvers alike are indebted to him for contributing to their intellectual history by creating universal frames of reference for their ideas through his application of the universality of logic and philosophy.

I would like to close this work with a note on Ṭūsī's approach to the political circumstances of his time and his choice to betray his Ismaʿili patrons and seek support from the Mongol invaders. Far from trying to exonerate him of opportunism and disloyalty, I would like to view his political choice in a different light. Ṭūsī managed to direct the energies of all those in political power at his time towards creating an opportunity for scientific progress and intellectual collaboration. In other words, he put these energies at the service of knowledge and of the greater good. Whether this was his intention, or he simply followed a natural disposition for survival, the outcome of his choice was positive and his contributions to knowledge were to benefit generations after him.

Chronological Table of Naṣīr al-Dīn Ṭūsī's Life

Date	Biographical events	Historical events
1201	Ṭūsī's birth in the city of Ṭūs	
1209		Death of the Ashʿarī theologian Fakhr al-Dīn Rāzī
1210		End of the 46 years of the Nizārī phase of *qiyāma*
1213-1221	Studies in Nishāpūr	
1221-1226	Studies in Mosul	
1217		Muḥammad Khwārazmshāh's campaign against Baghdad
1218		Birth of Hulagu Khan
1221		Genghis Khan crosses Oxus and conquers Balkh
1225		Death of Caliph al-Nāṣir
1227	Enters the Nizārī's service in Quhistān	Death of Genghis Khan
1235	Completed *Akhlāq-i Nāṣirī* in Ethics and Politics	
1243	Completed *Rawḍa-yi taslīm* in Ismaʿili philosophy	
1246	Completed *Asās al-iqtibās* in logic	
1247	Completed *Taḥrīr kitāb uṣūl al-hindisa li Uqlīdus* on Euclidian geometry	

1247	Completed *Sharḥ al-Ishārāt wa'l-tanbīhāt* in logic and philosophy	
1256	Enters Hulagu's service	Hulagu entered Persia through Khurāsān
		Collapse of the Nizārī fortress
		Death of last Nizārī imam, Rukn al-Dīn Khurshāh
		Beginning of the Ilkhānīd rule in Persia
1258	Witnesses the fall of Baghdad	Fall of Baghdad to Hulagu
	Wrote a letter of victory on Hulagu's order	Execution of Caliph al-Muʿtaṣim
1259		Begins the construction of Marāgha Observatory
1261	Composed *Tadhkira fī ʿilm al-hay'a*	
1265		Death of Hulagu; succeeded by Abqā' Khan
1270	Completed *Tajrīd al-iʿtiqād* in Twelver Shiʿa theology	
1274	Death of Ṭūsī in Baghdad	Death of Ṣadr al-Dīn Qūnawī
		Death of Thomas Aquinas

Bibliography

Adamson, Peter, *The Arabic Plotinus: A Philosophical Study of the Theology of Aristotle*, London: Duckworth, 2002.

Āmulī, Ḥasan H., *Āghāz wa-anjām-i Khwāja Naṣīr al-Dīn Ṭūsī: Muqaddama wa-sharḥ wa-taʿlīqāt*, Tehran: Chāp-khāna-yi Wizārat-i Farhang wa-Irshād-i Islāmī, 1374 S.H./1995.

Āmulī, Ḥaydar b. ʿAlī, *Jāmiʿ al-asrār wa-manbaʿ al-anwār*, eds., Henry Corbin and Othman Yahya, Tehran: Anīstītū-i Īrān va-Faransa, 1969.

Ansari, Hasan, Preface to *Talkhīṣ al-Muḥaṣṣal* by Khwāja Naṣīr al-Dīn Ṭūsī, ed. Hasan Ansari, Tehran: Mīrāth-i Maktūb, 2016.

Aydüz, Salim, 'Naṣīr al-Dīn Ṭūsī's Influence on Ottoman Scientific Literature (Mathematics, Astronomy, Natural Sciences)', *Intl. J. Turkish Studies*, vol. XVII, nos. 1 & 2, 2011, pp. 21–38.

Belo, Catarina, 'Freedom and Determinism', in Richard C. Taylor and Luis Xavier López Farjeat, eds., *The Routledge Companion to Islamic Philosophy*, London & New York: Routledge, 2014, pp. 325–336.

Black, Antony, *The History of Islamic Political Thought from the Prophet to the Present*, Edinburgh: Edinburgh University Press, 2011.

Chittick, William, 'Mysticism versus Philosophy in Earlier Islamic History: The Al-Ṭūsī, Al-Qūnawī Correspondence', *Religious Studies*, vol. XVII, no. 1, 1981, pp. 87–104.

Dabashi, Hamid, 'Khwājah Naṣīr al-Dīn Ṭūsī: the Philosopher/Vizier and the Intellectual Climate of his Times', in Seyyed Hossein Nasr and Oliver Leaman, eds., *History of Islamic Philosophy*, 2 vols., London & New York: Routledge, 1996, vol. II, pp. 527–584.

Daftary, Farhad, *The Ismāʿīlīs: Their History and Doctrines*, Cambridge: Cambridge University Press, 1990.

Fakhry, Majid, *Ethical Theories in Islam*, Leiden: Brill, 1994.

Fārābī, Abū Naṣr, *Mabādi' ārā' ahl al-madīna al-fāḍila*, trans. Richard Walzer as *On the Perfect State*, Oxford: Clarendon Press, 1982.

Haleem, Abdel M.A.S., trans., *The Qur'an*, Oxford, UK: Oxford University Press, 2016.

Ḥillī, Muḥammad al-Muṭahhar, *al-Jawhar al-naḍīd fī sharḥ manṭiq al-tajrīd*, ed. Muḥsin Bīdārfar, Tehran: Intishārāt-i Bīdār, 1363 S.H./1984.

———, *Kashf al-fawā'id fī sharḥ Qawāʿid al-ʿaqā'id*, ed. Ḥasan al-Makkī al-ʿĀmilī, Beirut: Dār al-Ṣafwa, 1993.

———, *Kashf al-murād fī sharḥ Tajrīd al-iʿtiqād*, ed. Ḥasan Ḥasanzāda Āmulī, Qom: Mu'assasa-i Nashr-i Islāmī, 1433 A.H.

Ibn Miskawayh, *Tahdhīb al-akhlāq*, trans. Constantine K. Zurayk as *The Refinement of Character*, Beirut: Great Books of the Islamic World Inc., 2002.

Ibn Sīnā, *Avicenna's De anima: Being the Psychological Part of Kitāb al-Shifa'*, ed. Fazlur Rahman, London: Oxford University Press, 1959.

Ibrāhīmī Dīnānī, Ghulām Ḥusayn, *Naṣīr al-Dīn Ṭūsī faylasūf-i guftigū*, Tehran: Hermes, 2007.

Iqbālī, Muʿaẓẓama, *Shiʿr wa-shāʿirī dar āthār-i Khwāja Naṣīr al-Dīn Ṭūsī*, Tehran: Sāzmān-i Chāp wa-Intishār-i Wizārat-i Farhang wa-Irshād-i Islāmī, 1370 S.H./1991.

Iṣfahānīyān, Dāwūd & Sāsān Sipanta, 'Risāla-yi az Khwāja Naṣīr al-Dīn Ṭūsī dar ʿilm-i mūsīqī', *Journal of the Faculty of Literature and Humanities at Tehran University*, nos. 138 & 139, 1370 S.H./1991, pp. 23–42.

Juwaynī, ʿAṭā Malik, *Tārīkh-i jahāngushāy*, ed. Muḥammad b. ʿAbd al-Wahhāb Qazwīnī, 3 vols., Leiden: Brill, 1911.

Kirmānī, Ḥamīd al-Dīn, *Maṣābīḥ fī ithbāt al-imāma*, ed. and trans. Paul E. Walker as *Master of the Age: An Islamic Treatise on the Necessity of the Imamate*, New York: I. B. Tauris, 2007.

———, *Rāḥat al- ʿaql*, eds. Kāmil Husayn and Muḥammad Muṣṭafā Ḥilmī, Cairo: Dār al-Fikr al-ʿArabī, 1953.

———, '*al-Risāla al-mawsūma bi'l-muḍī'a fi'l-amr wa'l-āmir wa'l-ma'mūr*', in Muṣṭafā Ghālib, ed., *Majmūʿat rasā'il al-Kirmānī*, Beirut: al-Mu'assasa al-Jāmiʿiyya li'l-Dirāsāt wa'l-Nashr wa'l-Tawzīʿ, 1983, pp. 113–133.

Landolt, Herman, 'Khwājah Naṣīr al-Dīn al-Ṭūsī, Ismaʿīlism and Ishrāqī Philosophy', in N. Pourjavady and Ž. Vesel, eds., *Naṣīr al-Dīn Ṭūsī: Philosophe et Savant du XIIIe Siècle*, Tehran: Institut Français de Recherche en Iran, 2000, pp. 13–30.

Madelung, Wilferd, 'Ismāʿīliyya', in P. Bearman, Th. Bianquis, C. E. Bosworth, et al., eds., *Encyclopaedia of Islam*, 2nd ed. (*EI2*), 12 vols., Leiden, NL: E. J. Brill, 1960-2005.

———, 'Naṣīr al-Dīn Ṭūsī's Ethics between Philosophy, Shiʿism, and Sufism', in Paul Luft and Colin Turner, eds., *Shiʿism*, 4 vols., London & New York: Routledge, 2008, vol. II, pp. 69–85.

———, 'To See All Things through the Sight of God: Naṣīr al-Dīn Ṭūsī's Attitude to Sufism', in N. Pourjavady and Ž. Vesel, eds., *Naṣīr al-Dīn Ṭūsī: Philosophe et Savant du*

XIIIe Siècle, Tehran: Institut Français de Recherche en Iran, 2000, pp. 1–11.

Mayer, Toby, 'Fakhr al-Dīn Rāzī's Critique of Ibn Sīnā's Argument for the Unity of God in the *Išārāt* and Naṣīr al-Dīn aṭ-Ṭūsī's Defence', in David Reisman, ed., *Before and After Avicenna: Proceedings of the First Conference of the Avicenna Study Group*, Leiden: Brill, 2003, pp. 199-218.

Meisami, Sayeh, *Knowledge and Power in the Philosophies of Ḥamīd al-Dīn Kirmānī and Mullā Ṣadrā Shīrāzī*, London: Palgrave-Macmillan, 2018.

Mīnāgar, Gholāmreza, 'Nigāhī bi naw'āwarīhā-yi falsafī wa-kalāmī-ya Khwājah Naṣīr al-Dīn Ṭūsī', *Faṣlnāma-yi ḥikmat wa-falsafa*, vol. 1, 2010, pp. 120–137.

Morewedge, Parviz, 'The Analysis of Substance in Ṭūsī's Logic', in George F. Hourani, ed. *Essays on Islamic Philosophy and Science*, Albany: State University of New York Press, 1975, pp. 158–188.

Naysābūrī, Aḥmad b. Ibrāhīm, *Ithbāt al-imāma*, ed. and trans. Arzina R. Lalani as *Degrees of Excellence: A Fatimid Treatise on Leadership in Islam*, London: I. B. Tauris, 2010.

Nuʿmān, Abū Ḥanīfa, *Asās al-ta'wīl*, ed. Aref Tamer, Beirut: Manshūrāt Dār al-Thaqāfa, 1960.

Pourjavady, Nasrollah, *Daw mujaddid: Muḥammad Ghazālī wa Fakhr-i Rāzī*, Tehran: Markaz-i Nashr-i Dānishgāhī, 2003.

———, 'ʿIrfān-i Khwāja Naṣīr dar *Awṣāf al-ashrāf*, in N. Pourjavady and Ž. Vesel, eds., *Naṣīr al-Dīn Ṭūsī: Philosophe et Savant du XIIIe Siècle*, Tehran: Institut Français de Recherche en Iran, 2000, pp. 39–56.

Raḍawī, Muḥammad Taqī Mudarris, *Aḥwāl wa-āthār-i qudwa-yi muḥaqqiqīn wa-ṣulṭān-i ḥukamā wa-mutakallimīn ustād-i bashar wa-ʿaql-i ḥādī al-ʿashar Abū Jaʿfar Muḥammad b. Muḥammad b. al-Ḥasan al-Ṭūsī mulaqqab bih Naṣīr al-Dīn*, Tehran: Chāpkhāna-yi dāwarpanāh wa khwājah, 1354/1976.

Ragep, F. Jamil, 'From Tūn to Turuń: The Twists and Turns of the Ṭūsī-Couple', in Rivka Feldhay and F. Jamil Ragep, eds., *Before Copernicus: The Cultural Contexts of Scientific Learning in the Fifteenth Century*, Montreal & Kingston, Canada: McGill-Queen's University Press, 2017, pp. 161-197.

———, 'The Two Versions of the Ṭūsī Couple', in *From Deferent to Equant: A Volume of Studies in the History of Science in the Ancient and Medieval Near East in Honour of E. S. Kennedy*, New York: New York Academy of Sciences, 1987, pp. 329–356.

Saliba, George & Kenney, E. S., 'The Spherical Case of the Ṭūsī Couple', in N. Pourjavady and Ž. Vesel, eds., *Naṣīr al-Dīn Ṭūsī: Philosophe et Savant du XIIIe Siècle*, Tehran: Institut Français de Recherche en Iran, 2000, pp. 105–111.

Schubert, Gurdun, *Annäherungen: Der Mystisch-philosophische Briefwechsel zwischen Ṣadr ud-Dīn Qōnawī und Naṣīr ud-Dīn-i Ṭūsī*, Beirut: Commissioned by Franz Steiner Publishers of Stuttgart, 1995.

Shehadi, Fadlou, *Philosophies of Music in Medieval Islam*, Leiden: E. J. Brill, 1995.

Shihadeh, Aymen, 'From al-Ghazālī to al-Rāzī: 6th/12th Century Developments in Muslim Philosophical Theology', *Arabic Sciences and Philosophy*, vol. xv, 2005, pp. 141–179.

Sijistānī, Abū Yaʿqūb, *Kashf al-maḥjūb*, trans. Henry Corbin as *Le Dévoilement des choses cachées*: *Recherches de philosophie ismaélienne*, Lagrasse: Éditions Verdier, 1988.

Suhrawardī, Shihāb al-Dīn, *The Philosophy of Illumination*, eds. and trans. John Walbridge & Hossein Ziai, Provo, UT: Brigham Young University Press, 1999.

Ṭūsī, Naṣīr al-Dīn, *Āghāz wa-anjām*, ed. and trans. S. J. Badakhchani as *Origin and Destination*, in *Shiʿi*

Interpretations of Islam: Three Treatises on Theology and Eschatology, London: I. B. Tauris and the Institute of Ismaili Studies, 2010, pp. 46–88.

———, *Akhlāq-i Muḥtashamī*, ed. Muḥammad Taqī Dānish-pazhūh. In *Akhlāq-i Muḥtashamī and Three Other Treatises.* Tehran: Tehran University Press, 4th edition 1339 S.H./1961.

———, *Akhlāq-i Nāṣirī*, trans. G. M. Wickens as *The Nasirean Ethics*, London & New York: Routledge, 1964.

———, *Asās al-iqtibās* in *Taʿlīqa bar Asās al-iqtibās-i Khwāja Naṣīr-i Ṭūsī* by Sayyid ʿAbd Allāh Anwār, 2 vols. Tehran: Nashr-i Markaz, 1996.

———, *Awṣāf al-ashrāf*, ed. Sayyid Mahdī Shams al-Dīn, Tehran: Sāzmān-i Chāp wa-Intishārāt-i Wizārat-i Farhang wa-Irshād-i Islāmī, 1369 S.H/1990.

———, *al-Bāb al-bāhiya fi'l-tarākib al-sulṭāniyya*, ed. and trans. Daniel L. Newman as *The Sultan's Sex Potion*, London: Saqi Books, 2014.

———, *Jabr wa-qadar*, trans. Parvis Morewedge as *Determinism and Predestination* in *The Metaphysics of Ṭūsī*, New York: The Society for the Study of Islamic Philosophy and Science, 1992, pp. 1–43.

———, *Miʿyār al-ashʿār*, ed. Jalīl Tajlīl, Tehran: Nashr-i Jāmī, 1369 S.H. /1990.

———, *Muṣāriʿ al-muṣāriʿ*, ed. Shaykh Ḥassan al-Muʿizzī, Qom: Maktabat al-Manshūrāt Ayatollah al-Marʿashī al-Najafī, 1985.

———, *Rawḍa-yi taslīm*, ed. and trans. S. J. Badakhchani as *Paradise of Submission: A Medieval Treatise on Ismaili Thought*, London: I. B. Tauris in association with the Institute of Ismaili Studies, 2005.

———, *Risāla fi'l-imāma*, ed. Muḥammad Taqī Dānishpazhūh, Tehran: Tehran University Press, 1335 S.H.